A Fool's Journey

A Fool's Journey

Walking Japan's Inland Route in Search of a Notion

William de Lange

Toyo PRess

For more on books by William de Lange visit:
www.williamdelange.com

First edition, 2018

Published by TOYO PRess
Visit us at: www.toyopress.com

ISBN 978-94-92722-05-8

For my brother John
who has always been there
through everything

I shall be telling this with a sigh
Somewhere ages and ages hence:
Two roads diverged in a wood, and I—
I took the one less traveled by,
And that has made all the difference.

— Robert Frost

Contents

Shiojiri
Shimo-Suwa
Seba
Niekawa
Narai
Agematsu
Suhara
Nojiri
Tsumago
Magome
Ochiai
Nakatsugawa
Inuyama
Kani
Ena
Kamado

● NAGOYA

Sensei

For months I had been pestering my teacher about the trip. Now the moment had finally arrived: we would be visiting the Walhalla of swordsmanship, the Toyota campus of Chūkyō University. Situated in the hills east of Nagoya, it was the epicenter of Japanese martial arts. He had arranged for us to attend a master class by one of Japan's oldest and highly ranked practitioners of Japanese swordsmanship, or *iaidō*, as it is called in Japan. Ever since I had taken up fencing during my time in Tokyo on a Japanese scholarship, I had heard of the campus, a place where the crème de la crème of the Japanese fencing world practiced their ancient and inscrutable art.

By the time we boarded the hired minivan on a crisp Sunday morning in spring I was brimming with anticipation. The first time I had seen an *iaidō* demonstration by an old practitioner at my dormitory in Tokyo's Seijōgakuen-mae, I was swept away. I was spellbound by the quiet grace, the effortless mastery with which he wielded his sword. Not the swashbuckling type of fencing you see in movies, but a calm, measured execution of techniques almost disappointingly simple in their deadly dedication to effectiveness.

As soon as the old man had finished I had gone up to him and, in my still very rudimentary Japanese, asked him if I could become his pupil. I was chuffed to bits when he said yes, especially when he turned out to be a descendant of the Satake, an illustrious clan of warlords who had ruled large parts of Japan's northern regions during the Warring States period. He said he lived nearby, only a few blocks down the road to Seijōgakuenmae station (I later learned he lived almost next-door to the great cineast Kurosawa Akira). If I showed up the following Tuesday at six, he would take me along to the local police station, where he practiced in a *dōjō* belonging to the station's kendo club.

For the next six months, we used to walk the short distance from his house twice a week, crossing the foot bridge across the Sen River, down to the old police station near the railway tracks. We would train for several hours, and on our return, he would sometime invite me in to show me some old document, or just have a chat over a glass of cold beer.

Now, after many years of practice, I was going to see at work a living legend: a ninth *dan hanshi*. It was a rare opportunity; there are just a handful of ninth *dan* practitioners (the tenth only being awarded posthumously). Only every so often is a teacher promoted to such exalted heights, either because of their old age or because of their contribution to the martial arts.

We reached the end of a narrow road that wound itself through the pleasant hills around Toyota. Oddly, though I lived in Chiryū, which was only a few miles south from here, I had never realized I was living so close to the epicenter of Japan's fencing world.

I felt like a character in a Bond movie, on his way to a dangerous appointment in some exotic location. Following my teacher's instructions, I had brought along my best outfit, the traditional trousered skirt, or *hakama*, and a jacket in the same black, silky material with my name embroidered in white. I could not afford, nor was I expected, to show up in the expensive silk attire in which the higher-grade practitioners would attend. That privilege, my teacher had warned me, was only reserved for the high-ranking teachers. Glancing sideways at me from behind the steering wheel, he said there would be many of them. It was not often that one could be in the presence of such masters.

A hush descended on the gathered devotees when the old master finally entered the large hall. He moved slowly, deliberately placing one foot in front of the other without ever lifting them from the polished floor. At last, when he had reached the center of the hall, he turned towards us and solemnly bowed. The gesture was immediately reciprocated by the entire assembly, the only sound the delicate rustle of their silk attires.

He began to speak slowly and solemnly as if invoking pages from the Japanese constitution. He reminded us of the unshakable foundations on which our art rested, how those rules were applicable to all martial arts, indeed, even to life itself. While speaking, he demonstrated how those principles affected the execution of a technique, wielding his sword with a steadiness and power that belied his age. Though feeble, his voice was clear and authoritative. It was obviously used to a lifelong career of instruction and edification.

A rush of goosebumps ran down my spine and I became self-conscious. I had read of people who had gone through a so-called synergetic experience, in which all the senses worked together to give one a sense of heightened awareness, an almost transcendental experience. I was sure I must be going through the same motions: the tempered light coming through the paper windows, the smell of clove oil, the sound of the sharp blade cleaving the cold air.

I was startled from my reveries when the old master suddenly raised his voice. 'Yet there is one fundamental rule, above all, to which you must adhere to attain true mastery, and that is: TIGHTEN YOUR ARSE, LIKE SO!'

Upon this, he squatted deep through his haunches, while uttering a protracted and guttural groan of such mournful intensity that I believed he must, in spite of himself, have vacated his bowels into his *hakama* right where he stood.

The whole episode had been a pretty accurate metaphor for

my general experience of Japan, and undoubtedly many other *gaijin* (aliens) who had made the mistake of landing with preconceived notions. But could it be otherwise? Was it possible to come to Japan with an utterly open mind—to simply tighten one's arse and not wonder: *what the hell am I doing here?*

The Japanese have become masters at promoting the exotic, mystical, tantalizingly enigmatic image first caught in the lenses of early Western photographers who visited the country towards the end of the nineteenth century: Felice Baeto, Raymund von Stillfried, Charles Vapereau, but also Japanese photographers like Tamamura Kozaburō and Kusakabe Kimbei. Shot on the eve of Japan's dramatic period of modernization, their images still breathe the atmosphere of Feudal Japan, even though most date from after the Meiji Revolution (1868), which spelled the end of Japan's feudal period. It is a small miracle that many of these iconic images still pertain abroad in spite of the modern-day debris.

Utilizing their unsurpassed talent for artful packaging, the Japanese have learned to present an image to the outside world that is carefully sanitized of their country's less attractive sides: the physical—let alone visual, auditive and chemical—pollution of the countryside, the exclusionist society, the bullying culture at schools, the cruelty towards animals, and the stunning banality of the utter and endlessly regurgitated trash that is spewed out from television screens into millions of family homes on a daily basis.

But I have to be honest: like so many of the young hopefuls who descended on Tokyo in the late eighties, I had been a willing sucker for the carefully nurtured romantic image Japan projects abroad. As long as I can remember I have been fascinated by Asia. As a child, I would dream away with the adventures of Kwai Chang Kaine (played by David Carradine) in ABCs action series *Kung Fu*. My first interest in Japan, in particular, was roused by Clavell's romantic romp, *Shogun*. When it was televised I followed the example of its protagonist, Anjin-*san*, and kept a notebook with all the day-to-day Japanese expressions he learned from his charming love interest. I had let myself be bewitched to such an extent that, by the time I was eighteen, I uncritically accepted the now so familiar clichés: of the tough samurai warrior ethic that, according to the pundits, could still be observed in the workplace; of the subservient geishas who could still be spotted in Kyoto's narrow streets, and were said to represent the epitome of Japanese femininity. Worst cliché of all was that of Japan's so-called uniqueness. Isn't every country unique in its own way?

These romantic notions were in no way cured when I entered university and took up Japanese studies in earnest. The language, especially the classical texts of an old and for ever vanished Japan, presented another mesmerizing world in which I could indulge my yearning for a bygone era. Far from setting us straight, the lecturers smiled benignly as they corrupted our minds—they were, of course, afflicted by the very same infatuation. I automatically assumed that, inhabiting such a wonderful place, the Japanese could only share my rosy view.

It was only later, when I had mastered the language and returned to Japan as a technical translator at a robotics factory near Nagoya, that the veil began to drop and it began to dawn on me that the average Japanese person was just as obsessed by sports, cars, sex, money, the mortgage, or how to operate the bloody remote control, as the next person. Still, had it not been for my youthful dreams, I would probably never have worked so feverishly for my plane ticket to Japan with pre-Gulf War Iraqi Airways.

Looking back, I'm sure similarly romantic notions were shared by many of the *gaijin* whom I met during those first exhilarating weeks in Tokyo as we spent our nights in Shinjuku's incredibly cramped but cheap little bars. Or, better still, the wonderfully luxurious *o-furo*, or hot bath, of the male wing of Iidabashi's youth hostel. Situated at one end of the second top floor of a high-rise building next to Iidabashi station, it was surrounded with a wall of glass windows overlooking central Tokyo. We felt as if we had already conquered the bright, endlessly sprawling city below us as we sat in the bath's piping hot water. Soaking, steaming and puffing, we grew red as lobsters while we shared our bewildering first impressions and, as if to tempt providence, expounded to each other how we would go about our individual successes.

Robert, a suave graduate from a well-to-do Boston family, was confident he would prove his worth in finance. Maurice, a tall black Englishman with a broad cockney accent but a languid, poetic way of moving, hoped to further his burgeoning career as a ballet dancer. Then there was Tony, a Canadian of Italian descent. Bald at the age of twenty, he wasn't really sure what he was going to do, though, like us all, he was sure he was going to make a success of it. There were countless others whose names I no longer recall, for the place, a first port of call for many a *gaijin* following their touchdown at Narita or Haneda airport, was and undoubtedly still is an eternal post of transit for the ambitious and the hopeful—a nutshell modern-day equivalent of New York's Ellis Island at the end of the nineteenth century.

Were it not for the strictly enforced time limit of three days, we would probably have stayed on at Iidabashi indefinitely. Instead, we were forced to move from hostel to hostel like urban nomads, which, in spite of the inconvenience, oddly seemed to add to our sense of progress.

I was intent on carving a career in music. I had already visited a number of the bigger music companies with a demo tape I had mastered back home on a four-track recorder.

As my stay protracted, the companies became smaller and smaller. So, by way of necessity, did my aspirations. Yet my intoxication with Japan only grew. Despite being the world's largest metropolis, Tokyo somehow had managed to retain a rural feel, even in some of its more central parts. One of the first things that struck me was the small railway crossings with their bamboo barriers painted in wasp-like colors. Yet it wasn't so much the exotic details. There was little of the regimented town planning seen in other large cities. Instead, the small houses were thrown together in an eclectic mix ranging from the beautiful traditional *irimoya* (hip-and-gable) style down to the blatantly modern. Yet somehow they managed to create a pleasantly harmonious effect, set off from each other by low walls or fences enclosing pretty gardens where dwellers tended to their proud collection of *bonsai*, plants in pots, or other carefully arranged shrubs and bushes. Nor was there any hint of the neglect and decay that mar so many other inner-city areas. The houses and gardens were exceedingly neat and tidy, while the narrow tarmac roads with their fresh white traffic markings were so clean it felt like you could sit on them without getting yourself dirty. Even the ubiquitous web of electrical wires that crisscrossed the streets overhead seemed to add to the homely feel of a place where, here and there, one could even find a small rice paddy among a cluster of houses.

The people, too, were pleasant. For a newcomer like me, it was most obvious in the way you were treated in public. At train stations, conductors took the time to guide you to the right train. And though not always smiling, at stores, the shop assistants would invariably bow when you entered the store. Once, doing some groceries at a small supermarket, I forgot a few yen's worth of change on the counter. I had already turned the corner some fifty meters away, when the shop assistant accosted me. Out of breath, she handed me the change and apologized for not having noticed earlier that I had forgotten to take it.

I loved the way the small restaurant owners welcomed you with *irasshai*! Or how the staff of sushi restaurants called out, '*o-aiso!*' when you stood up to pay at the counter. Though today also used by customers to ask for the bill, I was told it derived from the expression *o-aiso ga nakute, mooshi wake arimasen*, i.e., 'there is no excuse for my lack of civility' (*aiso*). It made you feel like you were part of the social fabric, an insider, even though, paradoxically, they would in the same breath address you with the words *gai-jin-sama*, or 'Mr. outside person.' It illustrated the lengths to which Japanese went to please, indeed pamper their customers—like the white covers on the headrests in taxis driven by hands in equally pristine white gloves.

I was happy, in short, just to hang on, no matter what it took, even though my budget (what with all the obligatory nocturnal 'networking') was being depleted at such an alarming rate that I would be running out of money within a few weeks, facing an ignominiously early return.

Now, some thirty years after I first set foot in Japan, and just into my fifties, I was going to walk the Nakasendō, or at least the largest part of, the old inland route from Tokyo to Kyoto.

I wasn't sure what I was looking for really. I had always wanted to walk the Nakasendō. A university friend of mine had done the old Tōkaidō route in full Buddhist garb while studying Buddhism. Stretching from Kyoto's Sanjō bridge to Edo's Nihonbashi, the five-hundred-odd kilometer road connected the old capital of Kyoto to the new capital of Edo (Tokyo). As such it was the most important among medieval Japan's five major traffic arteries: the Tōkaidō, the Nakasendō, the Kōshū Kaidō, the Ōshū Kaidō and the Nikkō Kaidō.

Ernest Mason Satow, an interpreter at the British Japan Consular Service during the last years of the Tokugawa Bakufu (Japan's last feudal military government), arrived just in time to see this finely tuned web of ancient highroads still operating as it had done for centuries:

> Ever since the third Tokugawa *shōgun* established the rule that each *daimyō* must pass a portion of the year in Edo, the great highroads had become important means of internal communication. Posting stations were established at every few miles for the supply of porters and baggage ponies, and at each of these were erected one or two official inns called *honjin* for the use of *daimyō* and high functionaries of government. Around these sprang up a crowd of private inns and houses of entertainment where *daimyō*, their retainers, and traveling merchants used to put up.

The Tōkaidō was the recognized route for all the *daimyō* west of Kyoto, and of course for those whose territories lay along it. Then it was the main route for the pilgrims who flocked annually to the sacred shrines in Ise, and was the means of access to many other famous temples; so that of all the roads in Japan it was the most frequented and the most important from every point of view.

By the nineteenth century the Tōkaidō, the Nakasendō, and their less famous siblings had become tourist attractions in their own right. Their popularity was fanned by woodblock prints from artists like Ando Hiroshige and Keisai Eisen, who immortalized scenic and famous sites in hugely popular series like the *Fifty-three Stations of the Tōkaidō* and later the *Sixty-nine Stations of the Nakasendō*.

Knowing just how much has been lost of the Tōkaidō, which skirts the now largely urbanized Pacific coastline, I wanted to see how much was left of the Nakasendō, which takes the inland route through the Japanese Alps. I was prepared for the worst, but secretly hoping to still find stretches of it intact.

If I was really honest, I had to admit I was still looking for that romantic image that had nestled itself in my mind's eye all those years ago. That image had to a large extent been colored by the woodblock prints of artists like Hokusai, Hiroshige and Eisen. They depicted a Japan untarnished by the pernicious influence of the West and its industrialization, its countryside enhanced by signs of the presence of a culture still in harmony with its surroundings: an arched wooden bridge across a stream, a *bezaisen* getting under sail in Kominato Bay, a solitary *tori-i* amid the cold snow at Seki, a *daimyō*'s entourage crossing the Sa River.

Departure

On the train to Tokyo, everybody was dead silent. Along the windows, on long benches breathing the faint odor of incontinent elderly, tired salarymen sat slumped. Women clutching large paper shopping bags stood near the doors, trying to keep their distance from the ever-lurking *sukebe* (pervert), as there was no women-only section on this local train. Even the youth lacked animation, not talking to each other, but staring into the screens of their smartphones, texting or playing some virtual game. The only voice was that of the conductor, monotonously droning up in his carefully nurtured nasal voice the stations at which we would be stopping before we reached the terminus of Chiba station.

Changing trains at Chiba I drew a can of hot milk tea from a *jidōhanbaiki* (vending machine). It was my favorite brand: Royal Milk Tea. The Japanese slogan, emblazoned around the can in classic golden lettering read: *Otona no kaoru miruku tea*, 'The milk tea fragrant of adults.' The first swig in six years—an odd mixture of sugar, artificial flavors and a distant hint of tea—took me straight back to Taitō Misaki, the lone cape on the Boso Peninsula's eastern shore, the place where I wrote my thesis on Japanese journalism while sustained by liters of the beverage a day.

I was studying at Waseda University on a scholarship of the Japanese Ministry of Education. Getting it hadn't been easy. Twice I had taken the grueling exam at the Japanese embassy in The Hague. The first time round, I had passed the written tests but failed miserably at the interview, which was conducted in Japanese. I had prepared for probing questions on why I wanted to study in Japan and how I planned to use my time at their considerable expenses.

Conducted into an imposing office, I knew I was in for trouble the moment the Japanese official came in and sat down behind his wide desk. Lighting up a cigarette on a Bakelite cigarette holder, he leaned back in his leather chair and took me in for what seemed like an eternity. Then he leaned forward, blew a puff of smoke in my direction and asked, '*Naze anata no toshi de mada daigaku ni iru'n desu ka?*' (Why are you still at university at your age?).

Taken aback, I mumbled something about *mawarimichi*, 'a detour.' It wasn't what he wanted to hear, and certainly not the way in which he wanted to hear it.

Yet it was true enough, though 'detour' was a bit of an understatement. Always playing outside, I already had bad marks in primary school. I distinctly remember being sent home in my last year with a note from the headmaster lamenting my poor performance. Cycling home, I was terrified of how my dad would react (my brother had once hidden his report behind a cupboard). I braved the storm, which turned out not as bad as I had feared. Worried, my parents made me do a proficiency test, which suggested I was good at practical things, making things with my hands. So they sent me off to do a lower vocational training: rudimentary electrical engineering. I did alright and after four years progressed to the intermediate level, but got stuck in the first year. So I switched to mechanical engineering.

For two years I managed to stay on the straight and narrow, but by the time I reached my final year I was spending most of the time making music in my four-track home studio. I had financed it by painting houses for a slum landlord in Groningen with my childhood best friend. It was good money, but it came at the grave expense of my assignments. Again I failed to pass. My teacher, an old man who had served in Indonesia, suggested I first do my apprentice year before resitting for my exams. It was the best advice. Sent off to a cardboard factory on the German border, the reality of what awaited me hit me like a ton of bricks. I felt as if I had ended up in some Siberian Gulag where one had to work in the faint hope of earning one's freedom. It was winter, and each day I would get up at six to catch an old cross-border German train to reach the border town of Nieuweschans. It was still one of those old trains, with small compartments with a tiny stove that failed to make a dent in the biting cold. The rest of the day I would usually spend under some machine, struggling in a thick, rotting sludge of papier-mâché to get some roller unstuck or replace a cutter. It was awful. Most of the plant's mechanics seemed to have turned off long ago and went about their work in a mental stupor.

Back at school, determined not to end up like them, I studied like I had never before. I still failed to develop an interest in the subjects, but simply learned all the formulas and whatnot by heart—anything to get away from the Damoclean sword above my head.

I passed with the best grades of my class, but before I could move on I had to enter the military—another huge obstacle.

I wanted to begin my pilgrimage of sorts at Inuyama and end it at Lake Suwa, thus carefully sidestepping the ugly urban sprawl that now lines the first and last hundred kilometers of the Nakasendō and has long since obliterated most of the Tōkaidō.

Taking the Tōkaidō Shinkansen from Tokyo to Nagoya reaffirmed me in my decision. What was once one of Japan's most historic and scenic routes has, in less than a century, been turned into an urban jungle that has spread from Tokyo to Osaka like a huge metastasizing cancer. Flashing by my window was a drab tapestry of suburban dwellings, flats, railroad tracks, electricity masts, chimneys, tarmac, billboards, parking lots, viaducts, tunnels, concrete encased hill-sides, concrete encased riverbanks, concrete encased shores, all thrown together with no apparent rhyme or reason and topped off with an endless assortment of randomly dispersed factories, industrial plants and refineries—a depressing sight if ever there was one.

Thinking back to my first impressions of Tokyo I realized how at odds my view of Japan had become with my first impressions. Was I growing cynical? But no. I was aware that I had perceived Japan through rosy glasses on my first arrival. I had also spent my first weeks in Japan in Setagaya, one of Tokyo's most pleasant wards. But it wasn't only that. Paradoxically, some of the suburban areas of Japan's big cities and its small towns are more pleasant than the 'open' countryside. This is especially true of the wide urbanized belt that now skirts Japan's east coast, where the ugliness has had the room to grow unhindered.

Back in Mobara, on the eve of my departure, I had watched a long documentary on the illustrator and children's books author Tasha Tudor, pottering about in her beautiful garden among the Vermont countryside. It was a typical NHK production, combining perfect photography, heavenly music and poetry-perfect prose narrated by a sweet-voiced woman to produce a viewing experience designed to enthrall. There is a lot of this kind of utopian porn on Japanese television lately, clearly catering to a growing thirst for something green, something natural, something real. Watching the verdant splendor of Tudor's small paradise on a big, high-resolution screen made me think of that brilliant scene in *Soylent Green*, a film set in a dystopian New York of 2044. In the scene, the last wish of the protagonist's old-aged friend before he is about to be euthanized is to see for twenty minutes, projected on a huge screen before him, scenes of earth's resplendent beauty as yet unspoiled by man. How long, I wondered, before this would be our reality—or had it already arrived?

Inuyama, then, would be a hopeful start amid the deluge of modernity. There I could visit Inuyama-*jō*, one of the dozen or so castles in modern-day Japan not refashioned from reinforced concrete. The castle dates back to the middle of the fifteenth century and as such is rightfully designated a *kokudama*, a 'national treasure.' It is also the only castle that, up until recently, was still in the private possession of the Naruse, a clan that ruled the Inuyama domain since the early seventh century.

At the top of the castle's *donjon* some elderly men were showing Japanese tourists the views. One was pointing out to a pretty young woman the distant cluster of high-rise buildings marking the center of Nagoya. Somehow she seemed more impressed with Nagoya's sky-scrapers than the castle. And somehow I understood. Only an hour earlier I too had been worshipping at their feet, drinking *frappe latte macchiato* in one of the chic establishments so in vogue with Japan's finely dressed army of office workers.

For its time Inuyama castle had been tall too. Sitting atop a high hill beside the Kiso River the balustrade around the upper tier offered a panoramic view of the surrounding land-scape, a now as gruesome sight as everywhere.

Only the majestic Kiso River, courageously elbowing its way through all the hideousness towards the Bay of Ise, reminded one of how beautiful the view must have been when the first Naruse Lord stepped out onto the balustrade of his castle to survey his domain four centuries ago. Now we only have the woodblock prints of Hiroshige and the like to get a sense of how mesmerizingly beautiful Japan was then. Instead of houses of prefab materials, wooden buildings with stuccoed walls and thatched roofs. Instead of the tarmac and concrete, a checkered pattern of rice paddies and vegetable patches. And instead of high-rise buildings of glass and steel, the occasional temple, or shrine, or castle atop a hill.

Much of Japan was like that just over a hundred years ago, when foreign travelers like Isabella Lucy Bird, John la Farge and Julian Swift Kirtland toured the country and became enchanted by the unique charm of the Japanese countryside and those who dwelled in it. What would Lord Naruse make of the way his modern-day countrymen have destroyed the face of his domain with such ruthless efficiency? His beautiful castle is now a small oasis in a desert of concrete, iron and tarmac. It is a poignant reminder to the modern Japanese of the ugliness they have wrought and in which they now have to live. Could I even hope to find some of that lost beauty along the Nakasendō—I was dying to find out.

Setto

As far as lodgings went, I was off to a bad start. Reaching Kani, I called a *ryokan* some twelve kilometers down the Nakasendō.

A man answered the phone and, though I hadn't yet spoken a word, he pronounced the name of his establishment so slowly and with such deliberation, that I felt he was able to detect I was a foreigner just from my breathing into the mouthpiece.

'There are still rooms free,' he said, but immediately followed this up with, 'Would you mind if I ask you various questions?'

I wasn't too keen really, but half intimidated, half intrigued, I consented.

Continuing in his deliberate tone, he wanted to know where exactly I was at the moment, what age I was and how I was traveling. I told him.

After a brief pause, he said his establishment was twelve

kilometers from where I was. He then proceeded to calculate out loud that, at my average walking speed of three kilometers per hour, it would take me four hours to reach him. The time now, he continued, was twelve o'clock. This meant that I would arrive at four o'clock.

I was beginning to lose enthusiasm for spending the night at his establishment but asked him what the price was.

Now he grew even more deliberate, spelling out the price like the person on the BBC's Shipping Forecast: 'nine—thousand—eight—hundred—and—forty—yen,—all—in.'

It didn't seem to me the most effective way to coax a customer into an expensive stay, but perhaps it was just that I wasn't Japanese.

What was the price without dinner and breakfast?

'No,' he said in a tone as if I didn't understand Japanese custom, 'the—*beddo*, the—*dinnaa*, and—the—*burekkufaasu-to*—are—a—*setto*.'

I had heard the word *setto* used in this manner before, but somehow it felt as if he considered all three items as pieces of matching furniture essential to the aesthetic integrity of his establishment. It was nonsense, of course. Most places are quite happy with guests who only stay to sleep. There is even a special word for it: *sudomari*.

I had made myself the promise that I wouldn't spend more than seven thousand yen a night, or else I might run out of money by the end of my journey. So I thanked him and said I needed to think it over.

There was little to think about really. The only alternative was a cheap business hotel in the center of Kani. But the town was such a drab affair that I decided to do some stealth camping in the nearby hills, not realizing I would pay dearly for my *gung-ho*, or should I say, *banzai* attitude.

I bivouacked on the peak of a 300-meter hill. The view was magnificent and the weather perfect, so what could go wrong? Indeed, I should be fine even if it rained. Preparing for my journey, I had bought a small tent the size of a body bag. I had been assured it wouldn't leak, which was true enough. It nevertheless rained. The first few hours were fine, but as it grew late and the outside temperature dropped, a thin film of condense began to form on the inside of the tent's thin fabric. Midnight passed and the film began to ooze small droplets. I lay on my aching back, looking on helplessly as the droplets grew and one by one gave way to gravity. By three o'clock the top of my thin sleeping bag was drenched and small pools of condense surrounded the one-inch thick foam mattress on which I sought to remain afloat. By four I had reached such a state of discomfort that there was nothing left for me to do than to pack up and move on.

Having risen early, I covered such a distance that by the next evening I had reached Saitō, the entrance to the first paved section of the ancient high road. Thus far, tarmac had spread its greasy tentacles up and into every country road. Now, huge boulders the size used in Japanese castle walls were sunk deep into the ground and arrayed with the same painstakingly precision to form a path that would last forever. At the steepest sections, they were staggered to create giant steps several meters deep. Wherever the path ran at odd angles with the mountain's slope, it was intersected at regular intervals by narrow gutters, carefully chiseled into long slabs of granite to transport rainwater across the path, from where it could continue on its downhill course.

It was at least ten more kilometers to the nearest village or town and thus I decided to brave another night in my body bag tent. At least my gear was now dry again. I had aired it in the playground of a small park where the various fixtures served as perfect washing poles over which to drape my soggy gear. Nearby, a granny was playing hide and seek with her granddaughter around a statue of playing children, all the while taking photographs with a small camera from around the corner in an attempt to capture an expression of surprise on the child's face.

I was hopeful this night would be better. I had changed tactics. This time I set up camp in the forest near Ishi Tatami. Here, I calculated, the temperature would drop less dramatically, thus producing less condense. I also opened all the vents to create as much draft as possible to disperse the moist air. For a while it worked, but then a bright flash, immediately followed by a deep distant rumble, announced approaching rain. In the end, it wasn't much, but enough to force me to close the vents.

And thus I once more had to go through the disheartening process of having to see in miniature the laws of nature by which seawater manages to eventually fall from the heavens—a fascinating phenomenon to observe, to be sure, but not for two nights in a row. They had been right: the tent didn't leak, but what with all the condense it was hard to tell.

Early next morning, after a brisk walk of fifteen kilometers, I reached Futatsu Ishi, the massive rocks marking the eastern entry to this section of the road. My muscles ached, and having had little sleep, I decided to take a break. I found a bus stop bench and, making my rucksack into a pillow, prostrated myself along its full length—there would be no passengers at this early hour, even in Japan. A glorious sun had come out, and as I basked in its warm early rays, I fell into a deep slumber. I was woken an hour later by birdsong; a small bird had alighted on my one raised knee and was singing its heart out. Was it because I was a *gaijin* that it had mistaken me for a piece of furniture?

Getting back on my feet, I decided to cut down to the Meitetsu railway station at Kamado. From there I could take the train to Ena, where I could probably get a good night's rest and pick up the Nakasendō again.

Along the way, I passed the *ryokan* I had called the night before. It didn't look very promising, abandoned even, and despite the hardships of the previous night I didn't regret having skipped it. As I passed it, I imagined rooms filled with carefully arranged sets of beds, diners and breakfasts.

Coffee

From the Nakasendō a straight road ran down into the valley to Kamado station. It was approaching ten, and when I saw a signpost 'Coffee 300m' at the foot of a road running up into the hills on the left I couldn't resist: I had gone too long without a proper fix. On my mobile app, I saw that a hiking path at the end of this road even provided a shortcut to the station below.

The cafe had only just been opened and the owners, a young couple, took great pride in their freshly-made coffee and home-baked bread. Though I like the gambler's rush of the *jidōhanbaiki*, after two days of overly sweet coffee and tea, I thoroughly enjoyed the rich, somewhat bitter aroma of the real thing. The bread, though still the spongy white variety, was good too, and it came with real butter.

After an hour and several refills, it was time to descend into town via the hiking path. On my map, it started in the backyard of a remote house farther down the road. Having reached it, I called out '*sumimasen!*' several times at the door to the kitchen, and though I heard somebody moving around inside, no one came out. By now I had put several kilometers between me and the main road, and my untrained muscles were aching like hell. So I decided to look around the yard in the hope of finding the wretched path. I couldn't find it.

Just as I began contemplating the uphill hike back to the main road, an old lady clad in an apron emerged from the back of the house. She eyed me with some suspicion, but when I explained what I was doing in her yard, her eyes lit up and she directed me to the shed. When we emerged on the other side, she pointed to a few rotten planks across a brook at the bottom of the yard. It was the path I was looking for. Born into a generation still used to traveling on foot, she hastened to add that it hadn't been used in decades, that I might get lost, as it was a long way down. But I knew how fastidious the Japanese are about getting from one place to another. When there are roadworks, they aren't content to just place a sign, but post a special traffic warden, whose sole occupation is to guide the oncoming traffic and pedestrians around this clear and present danger on their way to wherever they're going. The same dread of unforeseen obstacles lies behind the *gaido*, the young stewardess-like ladies who guide groups through the mazes that are Japanese big-city train stations.

So I set off along the old footpath. The farther I descended, the narrower it became. Not only that. Years of neglect had given shrubs and trees an opportunity to reclaim their space, while old trees that had toppled now rested their dead and weary limbs across the path in all directions. As a result, what had once been a decent path was now a vague trail through the densest of forests.

Clearly, the time had gone where most of the traveling and commuting was still done on foot. Where people once made a ten-minute walk through the woods to reach their neighbors, they now preferred the air-conditioned comfort of their SUVs. It might take the same time to get there, but why bother to walk if one can sit in a comfortable seat in an airconditioned car? There are plenty of hiking routes throughout Japan, perfectly manicured and maintained, down to long cramps driven into the muddy areas to keep the carefully laid rocks that serve as stepping stones from getting dislodged. Yet they are all recreational, not a serious means to get from one place to another.

Isomura-san

At Ena I got off the train and walked the few kilometers along the Nakasendō to what was once called Ōi-juku, the forty-sixth post town from Nihonbashi in Tokyo. Thankfully, time had not wrought the kind of damage seen elsewhere. A few old building in the *irimoya* tradition stood in the elbow of a short curve before the road cut through the hills towards Nakatsugawa. Through it one could still see Mount Ena in the distance as Hiroshige had seen it two hundred years earlier.

On my way back to the station I saw a small, elderly man with a kind face standing along the side of the road. He had come up from a little side road and had stopped when he saw me approaching.

'*Sugoi naa*,' (That's great) he said as I was about to pass him.

I stopped and asked what specifically it was that he thought *sugoi*.

'You, walking on your own,' he said.

Living along the Nakasendō he must have seen many a foreigner, so I explained the purpose of my own journey.

'So you're a writer,' he said, adding, 'Me too.'

Pleasantly surprised, I asked him if I could take his photograph in front of what I assumed was his house.

He laughed a wide, generous smile that revealed a set of poorly maintained teeth. 'Of course,' he said, 'But this is not my house. Come along and I will give you some of my books.'

His name was Isomura. His house stood only a dozen or so yards away on the other side of the road. It had a narrow garden with a patch of lawn largely occupied by a white sedan, its windows opened. He made me sit on a small rickety wooden bench in the shade while he went inside to bring me some grape juice, which he called 'grape fruit-juice.'

As he emerged he presented me with two of his books, a novel and a collection of poems.

I asked him how long he had been writing.

'Twelve years,' he said. 'But I'm an egg.'

I assumed he meant that, as a writer, he hadn't really hatched yet. But when I later looked at his biography (which every Japanese book has in its prelims), I saw that both of his books had won prestigious literary awards.

For most of his life he had been an English teacher. He explained how, when he and his wife got married, they had also made a vow that on his retirement he would become a writer. It was something he had already decided when at the age of eleven he had had a *gentaiken*, a formative experience.

In his case it had been a life-threatening illness that had made him question what he wanted to do with the rest of his life.

We came to talk about his time as a teacher, and why it was that so few Japanese really master English as a foreign language. He conceded the rigid education system with its emphasis on grammar and reading had something to do with it. Yet he still thought that essentially it was because Japan is an island country. It is an often heard explanation, but he had a nuanced take on it. It wasn't so much that Japan was an island, but rather that it lacked physical borders that shift and change with time. With it come new neighbors, helping to instill a sense of 'the other,' of the need to interact.

When it was time to go I asked him to stand in front of the low tree in the corner of his garden for a photograph.

I asked him what kind of tree it was.

'A *kaki*,' (persimmon) he said.

I commented on the similarity between the Japanese word for persimmon and the continuative form of the Japanese verb for writing, but he didn't seem to follow (or he privately thought it was a lame comparison).

I extended my hand to say goodbye, Western style.

For the briefest of moments he was confused. Then he grabbed my hand with both his hands and said, 'My fate is in your hands.'

He stood at the top of the road, waving goodbye and wishing me a good journey. Then I turned a corner and he was gone.

Izakaya

That night I stayed in the Ena *ryokan*, efficiently run by two kind ladies. I had a beautiful room with a view of a carefully manicured garden with bonsai trees and a rock pool. It was heaven. Only when you have slept rough for a few nights do you really appreciate the comforts of a warm, dry bed and a soothing hot bath.

After my bath, I went for a stroll through Ena and ended up in an *izakaya*, a tavern. I had almost forgotten how good they can be. I enjoyed a wonderful array of various *tempura* (they even had a cheese variety, though I didn't try it), washed away with draft beer against the pleasant backdrop of a rowdy bunch of young interns.

And once more I realized how pathetic Dutch cuisine really is. In fact, it doesn't really have an indigenous cuisine. The best Dutch restaurants traditionally serve French food. And though a number of new Michelin-star chef cooks are making a valiant effort to escape the gravitational pull of the mashed potato, the average restaurants are blissfully happy to present their clientele with endlessly boring varieties of the same old fare. I feel like screaming whenever I sit down and wistfully open the menu, only to find they serve the umpteenth variety of an already half-baked dish.

Endemic are the so-called *tosties*, French bread with cheese and ham, a poor copy of *croque monsigneur*. A close second is the *uitsmijter*, or 'bouncer,' again slices of bread, but now the cheese and ham are on top—a few fried eggs thrown in to help make the distinction. You can immediately tell a mediocre place by how prominently these two plates (one can't call them dishes) feature on the menu.

Most annoying are the places that want to make a modern impression, but can't bother to make the effort, and thus come up with new varieties of the same, such as farmer's *uitsmijter* (with brown bread), or the revolutionary '*tostie* Hawai,' toast with ham, cheese and, you guessed it, pineapple—from a can, of course.

It is disheartening, like the cake they serve with their otherwise very good coffee. You read correctly, 'cake,' singular. Lucky is the culinary pundit who happens on a cafe—as opposed to the *coffee shops* with their *space cake*—that serves anything else than the ubiquitous *appeltaart* (apple pie). Bill Clinton, a self-declared aficionado of this not even Dutch confectionary, should really uproot from his twenty-acre mansion in upstate New York and move to some town, any town in Holland. He won't be disappointed; *appeltaart* galore. No, for all those to whom the local cuisine is a serious part of their travel experience, it would be better to skip Holland on their European itinerary—except Bill Clinton, of course.

Revolutions

The next day I slept in—that is, I got up at eight o'clock, still four hours later than the average of my body bag nights. At the station I had to wait another half hour for my local to Ochiaigawa. Across the track, on the grounds of the Meitetsu Railway Company, a small group of employees in grey uniforms and blue caps were warming up for the day. Gymnastic music was playing from a weatherproof speaker attached to the side of the building, and the group was swaying arms and torsos to its staccato piano chords.

Getting off at Ochiaigawa, I followed a great thoroughfare away from the Kiso River so as to again pick up the Nakasendō. It was another hot day. The temperature had climbed to over thirty degrees Celsius, and walking on the simmering tarmac felt as if I were being fried alive. Heavy trucks thundered past, billowing thick clouds of diesel fume as they scaled the upward slope, while the deafening roar of their engines drowned out the sound of the river below.

It was only after I had rejoined the Nakasendō and was well into the woods that the profound difference between the old and new mode of traveling really struck me.

By now the countryside had altered markedly. I had left the Kiso River only a few kilometers behind me and was already entering a landscape that in an odd way reminded me of Austria and Switzerland. Even the houses, their wide, overhanging eaves casting dark shades around their beam and stucco walls, were reminiscent of chalets. They were set in a deeply verdant landscape that stretched far into the distance, towards the other side of the valley. Beyond towered the Japanese Alps, their snow-capped peaks contrasting sharply with a crisp blue sky above. Only the absence of cows grazing on grassy slopes and the almost startling presence of rice paddies in the level pockets and the valley below reminded me that I was in Asia, some nine thousand kilometers from home.

It is hard to describe the sense of relief that washed over me as, back on the old trail, I began to make out again the sounds of nature, the warbler, the Japanese cuckoo, the wind high up in the trees, a brook's rush down below. Among the trees the temperature dropped to a pleasant twenty degrees, while the fragrance of pine resin filled my nostrils. It struck me how stressful modern-day travel had become. If only the English hadn't come up with their bloody industrial revolution we wouldn't be in this mess today; no good can come out of a revolution.

Except of course when it is a Japanese one. I can still remember how the renowned sinologist Jonathan Spence, while giving a guest lecture at Leiden University, openly marveled at the transition of power during the Meiji Revolution. Compared to those in China, he confessed, it had been a true 'Velvet Revolution.'

In 1868 the old Tokugawa regime had made way for a government led by some two-dozen former samurai, their average age just over thirty-five. Keen not to make the same mistake as China and be ruthlessly exploited by the likes of the British empire, the new Japanese government set out to remold their country in the image of the West.

One mission after the other sailed from Japanese shores to learn from the foreign powers. Starting with the United States, they visited the United Kingdom, France, Belgium, the Netherlands, Germany, Prussia, Russia, Denmark, Sweden, Bavaria, Austria, Italy and Switzerland. Then, taking from all of these countries what they considered best for Japan, they began to reform its institutions, its military, its education system, its civil code and its political system. They were so successful in their endeavor, that by the end of the century Japan had gone from being a feudal, agricul-tural-based economy to being a constitutional democracy, as well as an industrial and military world power—a feat never before and never since achieved by any other nation.

Japan's attitude towards the West at the time was eloquently expressed by one of Japan's great statesmen and the founder of Waseda University, Okuma Shigenobu. Meeting with the American journalist Julian Swift Kirtland on the eve of the First World War, the then Prime Minister explained:

When Japan, after her centuries of hermitage, had suddenly either to face the West and to compete with you, or to sink into being a tributary and an exploited people, our greatest necessity in patriotism was to recognize instantly that in the physical and material world we had to learn everything from you. Our social, commercial and governmental methods were suited only to the organization of society which we then had. We discovered that your world is a world of commerce and competition, that the achieving of wealth from the profits of trade demands training, efficiency, ingenuity and initiative. Our civilization had not developed these qualities in us. We could only hope that we had latent ability. Furthermore, observation of you taught us to realize the value of physical power. We saw that mere superior cleverness and ability in the competition to live is not sufficient until backed by a preparedness of force. America was our great teacher and we shall never cease to be grateful. In the physical world we had everything to learn from you, and today we must constantly remember that we have only begun to learn.

Then he said something even more interesting, especially when one considered the course his country has taken over the following century:

> In a material way we can never pay back to you our obligation for having been taught your material lessons. But it may be that Western nations have put too great a faith in materialism and that they will arrive at the bitter knowledge that the fruit of life is death unless the faith of men reaches out for something beyond the material. Then, if we have humbly guarded our spiritual wealth, the world may come to ask the secret of our spiritual values as we went to you to ask the inner secret of your material values.

It was a noble idea, but I'm not too sure the Japanese have succeeded in guarding their spiritual wealth. As a hopeless romantic I also have mixed feelings about their race to catch up with the West. I admire the Japanese no end for their initiative, their refusal to be dominated by others. At the same time, had they only been a bit less eager, large parts of the Tōkaidō, too, might still be intact today.

Magome

I reached Magome early in the afternoon. It was hot now and I hauled up at the first place that sold ice cream. An old lady with a child-like smile tapped me a cone full of the delicious frozen cream, while her daughter gave me a large jug of ice-water to fill my flask.

Exactly a century earlier, Julian Swift Kirtland also walked this ancient route, an experience he recorded in his entertaining book, *Samurai Trails*. He and his travel companions, an English orthopedist and a Japanese friend of samurai descent, did the five hundred kilometer route in high summer, when temperatures reach for the forties and humidity double that. Donned in their orientalist dress and pith helmets, they had a hard time of it. It was the excessive heat that drove Kirtland to learn his first Chinese character: that of ice, *kōri* in Japanese. This traditional Japanese cold delicacy, which can still be found on restaurant menus around the country, is made of grated ice over which is poured a good helping of syrup. The old ice shops were marked by a flag with the Chinese character emblazoned on it, a sign the intrepid explorer soon 'learned to distinguish from incredible distances.'

Ice, in those days, was not easily obtainable, and often it had to come from afar. Visiting one of the ice shops along the route, Kirtland noted:

That the flag above the door had some definite meaning for the villagers began to be most evident. The shop was filling. Mob expectancy is contagious and we found ourselves waiting tensely with no clear idea what we were waiting for.

The shop was now quite full and all eyes were turned to the street. We heard shouts from the outside that were almost *banzai*s, and a coolie came running in. His face was aflame from the happy look of completed service. He was carrying a dripping block of ice in many wrappings of brown hemp cloth. I do not know how far he had come with the ice. Perhaps he had been to some station of the distant railroad.

The maid took her hands from her kimono sleeves and seized the ice. She pulled off the wrappings. Next she took a saw and cut off an end from the cake. Another maid re-wrapped the precious remainder in the hemp cloth and buried it in a pit dug in the floor. A third maid had been standing by with a board which had a sharp knife edge set into it. The first maid scraped the end of the ice cake over this inverted plane and shavings of sparkling snow fell into her hand. She packed this whiteness into two large, flat, glass dishes. She poured into the snow the effervescing champagne cider and brought us the 'adventure.'

Having enjoyed my own ice-cream, I strolled into town—or rather, climbed up into town. Magome is built on a slope of a hill. As a result its streets resemble a consecutive flight of steep slopes that must be a nightmare in winter.

At the tourist office I inquired for rooms in the next post town, that of Tsumago. The lady behind the counter, gifted with a machine-gun-like patter, expressed her skepticism of me finding a resting place any time soon, be it in Tsumago or Magome. The last years had seen a rush of foreign visitors. In the old days the town would be quite empty at this time of year. Only the odd literary pilgrim, keen to visit the birth-place of the famous author Shimazaki Tōson, would find his or her way to Magome. Now the place was inundated with tourists, and to stand a chance of staying, one had to book weeks in advance.

She offered to contact the Tsumago tourist office, but to no avail, every place was fully booked. I asked her if there wasn't some place in Magome where I could stay, be it only a dog house (I dreaded the thought of another night in my body bag). She looked stunned for a moment, but then broke into laughter. She suggested she'd call some of the cheaper places in Magome in the hope of finding one that had had a booking cancelled.

It was my lucky day; the very first place she called still had a vacant room. It was called Shirokiya, just down the street, the way I had come. I looked at the map she spread out in front of me and saw it was the place where I just had an ice-cream.

Miami Vice

At night cool air blew in through the half-opened *shoji* windows of my room at the Shirokiya, carrying on it uniquely Japanese fragrances. I could hear the sound of cicadas, and combined with the feel and smell of the *tatami* mats, I was transported back to my first days in Japan.

It had not just been a love for the language and culture that had led me to Japan; I had fallen head over heels for a Japanese girl. Naoko had been a former roommate of one of my fellow female students at the English faculty of Groningen University. When we met I had already taken up a Japanese language course, given twice a week by an energetic Mrs. Odaka during evening hours. I just loved the language, especially its fascinating writing system, an odd mixture of Chinese characters and indigenously grown syllabic scripts. It felt like I was learning a secret language in which only I and some one hundred and twenty million Japanese could communicate.

By the end of my first year I spent more time on Japanese than on my English studies, and when I met Naoko my mind was set: I was going to Japan. I wasn't just going to Japan, I was going to impress her by becoming the first foreigner to land a record deal upon arrival. I had prepared a demo tape with a number of tracks my Fin de Millennium project, including a cover of *Merry Christmas Mr. Lawrence* by Ryuichi Sakamoto, one of my musical heroes.

Naoko was less impressed. The first hint she wasn't that enamored with my roadmap to success was when she wasn't at the airport to await me with open arms. Instead, one of her friends stood at the gate to collect me, saying Naoko couldn't make it as she had to *work*.

Despite these setbacks in my private life, like a true artist, I pursued my professional career. Armed with my demo tape I visited one record company after the other, but for some strange reason their talent scouts weren't as enthusiastic about my music as I was. Though they showed me the courtesy of listening to my music, somehow none of them seemed very interested in my music but rather more in my personal story. They seemed intrigued to see what had driven this foreigner to think his music would appeal to the sensitivities of the Japanese ear. They were invariably polite to a fault, but in the end they equally politely declined, even though (or perhaps because) I wasn't always too polite myself. Writing my first letter home I described one such typical meeting:

Yesterday, I visited CBS-Sony, one of the biggest Record companies in Japan. The way you come in is by putting on a highbrow English accent and demanding to speak to the person in charge of A&R—being a foreigner really helps.

The man who helped me first could hardly speak English, so I wrote down in Japanese what he wanted to know.

Next a flashy, Don Johnson, *Miami Vice* type of guy came in, sat down, lit a cigarette and asked me, 'so Mr. William, what's your story?'

I politely told him that I didn't come to Japan to get my autobiography published, and maybe he should listen to what was on the tape.

This, however, didn't seem to interest him very much, as he kept on telling me how lucky I was that he just happened to speak English and wanted to know how on earth I had managed to get hold of his name.

I told him I didn't know his name and after some more talking he listened with a minimum of interest while the tape got stuck in the recorder on which it was played. He told me it didn't sound very appealing to him, which didn't surprise me, as his recorder had almost shredded my tape. He concluded our brief meeting by saying I had to talk to a person from the international department.

So I thanked him for wasting my time and looked up the man from the international department.

The man from the international department turned out to be a pleasant person, who spoke much better English. He told me that he couldn't help me, as I wasn't signed on yet. I first had to land a contract with the domestic department—which happened to be run by the Don Johnson bloke I had just spoken to.

Tea House

Halfway from Magome to Tsumago I passed a tea house. It was a traditional one, maintained in its original state by the township of Tsumago.

The caretaker was Matsubara-*san*, a middle-aged man dressed in the traditional dress of the tea house keeper, a large character for *cha* (tea) emblazoned on the back of his blue *haori*. He inquired about my journey, and soon we were talking about the old times. Then the average traveler, he told me, clocked some forty kilometers a day. At that pace it took them only two weeks to walk from Kyoto to the then capital of Edo (modern-day Tokyo).

For the *daimyō* and their large retinues it took longer. Under the Bakufu system of alternate attendance, they were required to spend one year in the capital Edo and the next year at home in their domain. Their spouses and children, meanwhile, would spend that year on the opposite side, virtual hostages of the Bakufu. By this ingenious system called *sankin kōtai* the Tokugawa shoguns ensured the loyalty of those who had fought against them in the great unifying Battle of Sekigahara of 1600.

Travelling by palanquin, their greatest obstacles were the many rivers. It was a deliberate strategy of the shogunate, Matsubara-*san* explained, not to build any bridges across the great rivers that had to be crossed to reach the capital, so as to prevent any rebellious army from reaching Edo before the shogunate could take military precautions.

And while the Bakufu allowed the use of ferries on wide waters like the Tama and Fuji Rivers, it forbade their use on other rivers. To cross these, travelers had to rely on so-called *kawagoshi ninsoku*, an army of laborers whose work it was to carry travelers and their luggage safely across the river. The fee they charged would rise with water levels. During the rainy seasons, when rivers grew too wide to be crossed, they would declare a *kawadome*, or 'river stop,' This meant that travelers were delayed for days, even weeks, forcing them to stay and dish out even more money on lodgings and food at the nearby post station.

Kawadome, then, was a perennial worry for the lords, especially for those whose domains were far removed from Edo. And not only financially—were they to arrive late in Edo there would be hell to pay...

At this stage in Matsubara-*san*'s account, a young couple entered the tea house. They, too, sat down for some tea and began talking to each other, in Dutch, so I said hello.

They introduced themselves as Corlette and Peter. They were traveling around Japan and due to return to Holland in a few days. They were a pleasant couple, easygoing and full of questions.

I told them about my journey and they seemed impressed. Had I traveled a lot, they asked.

I told them that the last time I had visited I had spent two month traveling the length of the country to photograph its many castles.

They seemed slightly amused. Was I perhaps from the north of Holland?

I said yes. Could they tell by my accent?

Not so much the accent, they said, inasmuch that I had dropped the Dutch equivalent of the plural 's' in 'months;' like most northerners I had said 'two month,' instead of 'two months.' They had both studied at my hometown university of Groningen, she labor law and he criminal law—it was how they had met. Living for several years up in the north they first noted how the locals had a tendency to swallow their plurals.

We laughed; I clearly couldn't escape my roots.

She gave me her email address, asking me to let her know when the book would go on sale. I said I would, assuring them they could have a signed copy If they were willing to represent me at court if ever I ran into trouble.

We laughed some more and shook hands as we parted.

Rule Britannia

The stretch between Magome and Tsumago was the most beautiful on my journey so far. A long footpath led up over the Magome Pass and down through a densely wooded forest of cedars and cypresses. Every now and then there was a small bridge across a stream or rapid, after which the narrow trail plunged back into the undergrowth. All traces of modern civilization by now had disappeared, and I imagined myself in a country still ruled by samurai.

On the last leg of the road to Tsumago, I passed a number of elderly English tourists. Despite the breathtaking scenery they were invariably engrossed in deep albeit casual conversations on petty domestic issues, as if they were out for a stroll in their own back garden—which is of course still their attitude to the rest of the world.

At a local inn serving healthy delicacies like *kakeudon*, *zarusoba* and *yama-kinoko sansai*, I overheard one of them ordering 'English tea.' She made it sound as if it wasn't so much the origin or type as the nationality of the beverage that mattered. As she drank her tea she burped, which made me think of my spinster aunts from England who would do the same whenever they visited my mother in Holland.

Having toured the village, I revisited the inn for a coffee. It was almost empty now, except for a slender Japanese woman in her thirties wearing a long blue summer dress and a white hat fit for Ascot. She sat with her back towards me, studying the screen of her iPhone.

A few minutes later a Western woman came in. She walked straight up to the young woman and began complaining about the local food on offer, as a child would to her mummy. She had been to most places, she said, but none of them had 'a decent piece of meat.'

The young woman, obviously a travel guide, intoned a voice of motherly concern and began to suggest various alternatives, none of which seemed to satisfy the woman, who went on to complain that the last piece of meat had been quite 'chewy,' pronouncing the word as if it was a medical condition.

Having vented her spleen, she went to the toilet, when a bald man roughly her age ducked under the shop's *noren* (shop curtains) and also addressed the young woman. His tone was more that of a patient granddad, though the thrust of his message was the same.

His concern was the fat and sugar content in the food on offer. He had trouble with the 'pools of fat,' in which the meat 'floated.' Usually, he explained, there was a buffet at the hotels at which they stayed, but now he had to choose dishes he had never hear of.

It was a 'good thing, though,' he hastened to add, as he was now forced to eat 'real Japanese food.'

'Then what do you usually eat?' the young woman asked, the faint trace of exasperation hidden behind the veil of her exotic Japanese accent.

'Oh, vegetables, dry vegetables,' he replied, 'not smothered in some sauce.'

Tsumago

My immediate concern now was to find a place to sleep for the night. Along the quiet stretches through the woods I had noticed small posts with large bronze bells, as you would find on a schooner, sturdy, woven ropes attached to their clappers. At first I assumed they were there for the pilgrims. I had seen one man dressed in white solemnly sound one three times, each ring interspersed with a long pause before he continued on his way. Then, a few kilometers farther up, I spotted another bell, this time with a small notice. I drew near and read it. It said, 'Please sound the bell hard to scare away the bears.' Now I had two good reasons not to fall back on what might truly end up being my body bag.

Reaching Tsumago's outskirts I called at the very first hostel I found. But it was Saturday and the place was fully booked by a group of painters. The owner offered to call around for me. I thanked him. He shrugged, saying, 'Don't they say humanity is one big family?'

After making some calls he found a place for me. At eleven thousand yen the Fujioto *ryokan* was at the high end of the price range. Noting my concern, he added it probably had the best reputation in Tsumago.

I nodded but should have been forewarned.

Intercepting me at the entrance, Fujioto's landlord looked like a Japanese politician: he wore the aloof and cold poker face of those in charge of all high-end establishments. He bluntly told me that they did not cater to guests who only wanted a place to rest. I had better look elsewhere. His whole message was delivered with not the slightest trace of compassion, not the faintest hope of compromise—were I to be devoured by a bear on his doorstep that very night, I was sure he wouldn't bat one of his drooping eyelids.

As a last resort I visited the local tourist office. They found a place for me outside of town at half the price charged by Fujioto. It was three kilometers back along the road I had come, but the owner generously offered to pick me up at the tourist office at four, which left me with ample time to explore Tsumago.

The landlady was a not unattractive bespectacled woman, probably in her early sixties. She had a somewhat brusque manner—a farmer's no-nonsense attitude. But as I settled down behind the low table (*kotatsu*) in the guest room and engaged her in small talk she opened up. She disappeared to the other side of the house and reemerged with a small tray with green tea and *senbei*, as well as a small plate with a banana and a local delicacy called *hōba mochi*, a rice ball filled with sweet bean paste wrapped in a leaf of the Magnolia (*hōba*) tree.

To save costs I had asked for lodgings without dinner and breakfast, but soon afterward she came in with another tray, this time with home-made *onigiri* and a bowl of steaming *miso* soup. I thanked her and we came to talk about local food.

She grew most of her vegetables herself, she said, some ten varieties in all.

As she was speaking, an old man shuffled past the veranda in his pajamas. She looked at him with concern, as if wondering where he was going this time.

It was her father, she said. Then, with some pride, 'He's ninety-four. It's just the two of us now, him and me. I look after him, till my vegetable patch, and run the hostel.'

I said it must be hard work.

'Yes,' she said, now with even more pride. '*Erai deshō!*' (It's noble, isn't it?).

Yes, I said, it was noble.

We grew silent for a while, as we both looked at her small patch of vegetables outside. Then my phone rang. It was my partner. And as we talked I felt how blessed I was to have her.

The next morning, after a breakfast of toast and coffee, I made ready to leave.

I asked her again about the *hōba mochi*. Did she pick the Magnolia leaves herself?

'Yes,' she said. 'Come, let me show you.'

She walked ahead of me down the narrow road leading back to the Nakasendō.

After a hundred meters or so she left the road and walked over towards a few trees with large, fan-sized leaves. Plucking one of them she crumpled it up and gave it to me. 'Smell that,' she said.

It had a pleasant smell.

'It gets stronger when you steam them,' she said. 'It also has a preservative quality,' she added. 'It keeps bacteria out.'

I asked her to stand under the Magnolia tree and took her picture.

She put up her hand and made the popular V-sign, saying, 'It feels like I'm in high school again,' and laughed.

I thanked her for her hospitality.

Then we bowed and parted ways. I looked back, but she didn't. She was briskly walking back up the road, back to her father, her hostel and her vegetable patch.

Dean

On the stretch from Magome to Tsumago, I had frequently come across a man some ten years older than me. He wore a red T-shirt and a baseball cap. He didn't seem the chatty type so I didn't bother to strike up a conversation. On my way to Nagiso, I climbed up to the ruins of Tsumago castle to see what was left of it (nothing) and get a good view of the Kiso Gorge, which it used to guard.

I had dropped my gear in the wooden outlook and was drinking some water when I heard some rustling along the narrow path by which I had come. It was the man in the red T-shirt. This time we could not avoid each other.

He seemed to have reached the same conclusion, for he approached the outlook and said, 'Shame so few old castles are left.'

The ice was broken and we began exchanging travel experiences. He too was doing the Nakasendō, walking just the nice bits.

We agreed how beautiful this stretch still was and inevitably the conversation drifted towards how ugly much of the rest of Japan had become. We wondered how the Japanese put up with living in small, cramped apartment blocks, the only nearby space a parking lot filled with cars. Here it was different; the houses were spacious and in most parking lots stood at least one expensive car, which made him wonder how the locals made a living.

I asked him what his name was.

'Dean,' he said. He was from Adelaide. Usually he traveled with his wife, but this time around he was doing the Nakasendō by himself, like me. Back home it was still quite cold. When he had chatted online with his wife the previous evening she had been 'all huddled up,' he said and chuckled while a grin spread across his tanned face.

He had seen a lot of Japan, including the southern island of Kyushu.

I asked him if he had visited Kumamoto castle, which had been severely damaged by the recent earthquake.

No, he hadn't. He did visit the Chiran samurai district, but had been washed away by intense rain, at which point he had decided, 'Fuck this I'm going back to Kagoshima.'

Kiso Gorge

Around noon I reached Nagiso. From there the Nakasendō again followed the Kiso River, pretty much up till Shiojiri, some eighty kilometers upstream. It was hot now and I craved some refreshment. The cool orange juice from the Seven Eleven was nice, but I needed something more.

So when I reached Nagiso's outskirts I decided to take a plunge in the river. This was not as easy as I thought it would be, as there was a twenty-meter vertical concrete drop from the road to the river.

At length I reached a quarry, where a gravel path led down to the riverbed, if one could call it that. The river at this stretch consisted of huge boulders the size of cars, bleached bone-white by an unforgiving sun. Scattered among them lay huge tree trunks, lamp posts, truck tires and even a fifty meters length of electricity cable the caliber of my wrist. At one place the root end of a tree had been trapped between the boulders. The force of the river had pushed the heavy trunk up so that it stood erect again, as if it would presently spring into life.

At the gorge's lowest level the river's restless water rushed around and over the boulders and poured into a wide emerald pool.

I put on my swimming trunks and immersed myself. The water was ice-cold, but in the sweltering heat it was refreshing and soothing.

The place seemed so good that I began to contemplate setting up my little tent on a narrow strip of white sand on the opposite side. I would have to wade waste-deep through the ice-cold water, but my rucksack was watertight, so that wasn't a problem.

But it was still early, just past noon. If I wanted to reach my destination without the help of public transport I should at least plod on a bit longer.

And thus I climbed back up to the busy high road and continued towards Jūnikane, some six kilometers farther up along the Kiso Gorge.

I had only done a few hundred meters when I passed a huge signpost along the side of the road that read:

WARNING!
Please pay attention!
There is a dam three kilometers upstream.
Occasionally excess water is discharged downriver,
causing water levels to rise in a short time.

Clearly, camping alongside the river hadn't been such a good plan. I imagined myself as an older, hence more fool-hardy, version of Christopher Johnson McCandless, the real-life protagonists of John Krakauer's brilliant book *Into the Wild*. Like him I was laboring under the illusion that I had come well-prepared for my journey, only to realize my one fateful mistake as I was being swept downstream amid a deluge of trees, lamp posts, car tires and electricity cables.

Hotel California

After all the splendor of Magome and Tsumago, I quickly grew tired of the asphalt, the fumes, the noise of the high road. Just before I reached Jūnikane, I crossed a bridge over the river and followed a scenic inland route that would eventually lead me back to the river at Nojiri.

That night I stayed in a *minshuku*, which is a Japanese bed and breakfast. But this one didn't at all have the personal feel of a *minshuku*. It was a misnomer really. Though it had the Japanese-style rooms, they were hidden behind thick metal doors along a long, carpeted and narrow corridor one would expect in a business hotel.

The place was run by a woman who seemed more fit for a *snakku*, a kind of bar where bored and lonely middle-aged men have their name attached to their own whiskey bottle and are entertained by the landlady with karaoke, while they pester her with suggestive talk. She had all the social skills and thick skin to effectively deal with difficult customers.

Her sidekick was a diminutive, Quasimodo-like creature who felt free to talk down to me just because I wasn't Japanese. He ordered me to follow him down the narrow corridor. I slavishly followed, while the refrain of *Hotel California* distantly echoed in the back of my head.

For just the briefest of moments I thought he wanted to engage when he muttered I was tall.

Then I realized my folly when, having reached the end of the corridor, he pulled open a drawer and began rummaging among several neatly folded piles of *yukata*.

'There,' he said, still more to himself than me, 'that should fit,' and without looking at me he handed me the garment.

The place's only redeeming feature was the *o-furo*, which was completely done in *hinoki* (Japanese cypress) and had a commanding view of the mountains. I was—who would have thought—the only guest in the whole facility and spent half the evening soaking in the hot bath on my own in quiet meditation.

Compared to this place the Shirokiya at Magome had been so much nicer. It was slightly the worse for wear, but had all the more atmosphere. There the rooms weren't wall-papered with vinyl, but still stuccoed with *shikkui*, the traditional plaster made from eggshells, which is an art in its own right. And there the wooden beams were real, not veneered planks glued against what felt like concrete walls. Two sets of sliding doors had connected the rooms to a wide hallway, its floor made of thick planks. On the room side there were *fusuma*, but facing the hallway were simple *shōji*, their latticed structure uncovered with paper. There were no locks, no spying holes. The *shōji* were just enough to convey a need for privacy, without making one feel locked out. This gave the place such a feel of openness that I could only marvel at the idea. Of course in most parts of the world, such a concept would be utterly unworkable. Were one to run a hostel like this in Amsterdam one would be out of business before the month was out.

The next morning I realized I had been a bit harsh on the assistant. As I checked out he asked where I was going.

I told him I was headed for Shiojiri.

Did I know there was a shortcut back to the Kiso River? It was a just narrow trail through the woods, but it took one farther upstream, to where I could cross the bridge to Nojiri.

I thanked him and said I had enjoyed the *o-furo* and its beautiful view.

'It's good isn't it,' he said, 'it takes your tiredness away.'

Inabashi

That afternoon, on my way to locate the old bridge over the Ina River at Okuwa, I fell in with an old lady. I had already spotted her at the Nojiri train station, wearing one of those wide, cotton caps with floral patterns typical of country folk.

She asked me where I was going.

I said I was walking the Nakasendō and was looking for the old bridge across the Ina River.

She said it had long gone. There was a new bridge across the river now and we would reach it presently.

I asked her whether she lived in Okuwa.

She didn't. She just went shopping at its new supermarket, as her own village didn't have one anymore.

Was the drain of people bad around here?

'Not too bad,' she said, pointing to a big building on the other side of the river. 'At least we have the plant that makes car parts, so most young people here have jobs.'

It was worse deeper among the mountains, where the flight of young people towards the big cities conspired to create ghost villages inhabited by only a handful of elderly.

By now we had reached the bridge. In parting she complimented me on my Japanese. I told her I had worked as a technical translator in nearby Aichi prefecture.

'Oh, that's alright, then,' she said, 'you'll be fine.' And with that we bowed and went our separate ways.

After the bad experience at the *minshuku* the previous night I decided to brave my tent once more. I set up camp a few hundred meters upstream from the bridge we had crossed. The spot was near idyllic, a narrow strip of white sand bordering a shallow pool among the rocks. There were also no dams upstream, so I wouldn't be washed away in my sleep.

I had bought myself some sushi and *yakisoba* at the supermarket and, like a pro, I had hung the bag in the cold water by a twig to preserve its content. The next time I looked the twig was straining with the weight: water had leaked into the bag and the sushi and *yakisoba* were drenched—so much for my survival skills.

Shinano-san

The next morning I woke up at half past four, cold and shiv-ering. It seemed nothing I did could make sleeping rough a comfortable experience—though it did occur to me that perhaps it was why it involved the word 'rough.' I packed up my gear and walked down to the big supermarket, where I scored a hot coffee from a line of vending machines.

From there I climbed back into town to photograph the Kashima shrine, on Suhara's northern outskirts. This is where Hiroshige drew his evocative wood-print painting of travelers seeking refuge at the shrine from the rain.

While I was photographing a huge cedar tree that was already there in Hiroshige's time, an old man in a mini truck pulled up. Dismounting from his small cabin, he took two canisters from the back of his truck and crossed the road to a small brook just beside the tree. There he filled his canisters from a basin into which the brook cascaded. He wore an old pair of trainers, stringless boots and was clad in one of those webbed jackets with sewn-on pockets worn by sports anglers.

Then he spotted me and, his dripping canisters still dangling from his hand, asked me where I was going.

I said I had come to photograph the same scene depicted by Ando Hiroshige.

It didn't seem to ring a bell. He raised the sun-shade of his cap as if to think more clearly, but it didn't help. '*Aaah, yoku wakaran naa,*' (Well, don't know about that) he said, as a helpless smile spread across his tanned and weathered face.

I asked him if the water was potable.

No, he said, it was for his vegetable patch, which was on the other side of the valley.

'Have you got time?' he asked.

When I said yes, he put the canisters in the back of his truck and beckoned me to follow him. I did, and as we walked down towards the village, I asked him what vegetables he grew.

Kyūri (gurkins), *nasu* (eggplants), *sansai* (mountain vegetables), he said.

Did he use pesticides?

He looked up at me in surprise and replied with an emphatic 'No!'

By now we had again entered the outskirts of Suhara and, walking up to an old house, he drew open the front door and let me in.

A narrow, cluttered hallway led to the back of the house.

On its left side were *shōji* that gave way to a small living room. The wall on the other side was hung with dozens of framed photographs, many of mountain flowers, but also of groups of people and a few with the old man in younger years atop what was clearly a mountain's summit.

His name was Shinano Nobuo. He had lived here all his life and was eighty-four.

I asked him about the photographs; had he made them himself?

He said yes. All the flowers had names that began with the same three syllables as his family name, 'shi-na-no.' He had taken them on his many forays into the mountains.

Was he a mountaineer then?

No, he'd been part of a group maintaining the hiking routes around Suhara.

This was heavy work. On my hikes through the mountains, I had seen how meticulous these paths were maintained.

He had climbed the eighteen hundred meters high Itose-*yama* on several occasion. The last two times had been with his grandchildren, first his granddaughter, then his grandson, both occasions proudly on display in his home-made gallery.

Then I saw there was a photograph of the Kashima shrine from the exact same angle I had taken my picture just a few minutes earlier. Next to it was one of the Inabashi, the bridge I had crossed with the old lady the day before.

For a moment I wondered whether Shinano-*san* was perhaps growing forgetful.

Then I read the caption of the first photograph. Written in beautifully calligraphic characters, it said: 'Suhara-juku by Eisen.'

Of course! There was nothing wrong with his memory, but all the more with mine. I should have remembered that the *Sixty-nine Stations of the Nakasendō* was a joint venture. Following the success of the *Fifty-three Stations of the Tōkaidō*, Hiroshige had collaborated with another great wood print artist, Keisai Eisen, to give the inland route's post stations a similar treatment. (Researching the matter on my return home, I found that this particular image was not done by Eisen, though the one of Ina bridge was.)

The upper ledge around his tiny living room was crammed with certificates.

I asked Shinano-*san* what he had done to receive them.

Taking his time, he proudly explained. The central one was for helping to reach the municipal's can-collection goal, thus helping to clean up Japan's heavily polluted roadsides. He had received it in person from the prefectural governor, who had treated him like a friend, he said.

The one next to it was for his work to promote traffic safety. Then there were several cases with medals and ribbons for his service in the local fire brigade.

'When I was young there wasn't a house in the village that didn't at least contribute one son to the brigade,' he said. 'Now all the young people have left, so the average age of the volunteers keeps on rising.'

We were still only halfway around the room; clearly Shinano-*san* had done his bit for the common good.

As we were talking a feeble, high-pitched voice called out from the other side of the *fusuma* that separated the front room from the rear of the house.

'Who's that you're talking to? Why don't you rest a bit?'

Slightly irritated, Shinano-*san* slid open one of the *fusuma*, leaned against it and called out, 'I'm not done yet. I just need to water the vegetable patch.'

There was a faint rumbling on the other side and more muttering, not so much complaining but imploring.

Smiling embarrassedly, he stepped back into the room and was about to resume his exposition, when a terribly frail old woman stepped into the opening. She was in her pajamas and can't have been much taller than one meter twenty; she just reached her husband's shoulders even though he barely reached mine.

Holding on to the *fusuma* with her right hand she began apologizing profusely and continued to reproach her husband, all the while gesturing in front of her face with her trembling left hand, as if to wave away a fly.

'He's just so spirited,' she lamented. 'He won't sit down for a moment and take some rest.'

As she was talking her husband bent over and leaned with both hands on one of the low sitting chairs and softly groaned, though I couldn't tell whether it was out of exasperation with his wife or out of plain fatigue.

When she had finished he raised himself again and smiled sheepishly.

At this point she offered to bring in some tea. But I didn't want to impose myself on them any longer. So I thanked them both for their hospitality and, having taken a photograph of Shinano-*san* proudly standing in front of his old house, I took my leave.

Are You a Saboteur?

I was touched by the domestic scene I had just witnessed: it seemed heroic and pathetic at the same time. Especially the old woman had touched a nerve in me. The childlike innocence on her angelic face reminded me of my mother in her last year, playfully dangling her legs from the bed as I fastened her pajamas for the night.

Once these frail old women had been young girls full of life, eager to find out what the future had in store for them.

In my mother's case, life had been quite adventurous. The youngest of three sisters she had signed up for the Navy's Fleet Air Arms at the age of seventeen on the outbreak of World War II. After the war she had joined the Land Army, followed by a short stint at a telephone exchange in London, until she had eventually signed on as a stewardess on the merchant ship Langley Clyde and met my dad.

When she entered the Fleet Air Arms, she was selected to be an airplane electrician and, after several months of training near Inverness, posted to the Royal Naval Air Station of St Merryn, near the fashionable seaside resort of Padstow.

One of her favorite anecdotes was when she had checked the ignition of an airplane, but failed to first disengage some lever. It had caused the plane's propeller to tear right through the wood and canvas fuselage of a nearby parked Spider Moth. She was called in for questioning by her commanding officer, who asked her, 'Are you a saboteur?'

A few months ago I was visiting one of my few surviving English relatives, Pat, her favorite cousin, who had been going through family photographs and letters in her deceased mother's possession. She showed them to me one night and produced from the bottom of the shoe box a small envelope. It contained a letter my mother had sent to her eldest sister shortly after she had arrived in Padstow. Death rates among pilots flying missions over occupied Europe and Germany were notoriously high. But from her letter it is clear that the young men were at risk the very moment they boarded a plane:

We have been very unfortunate on the squadron lately. We have had about six crashes in just over a week. Two of the planes went into the sea. One was a Martinet and I had done the inspection on it that morning. It crashed into the sea but the pilot & air gunner managed to escape. I was so glad! The pilot was cut up quite a bit. I saw him today on the squad:

he first came to see them. I asked him how he felt and he said not too bad, except for feeling dizzy in the head. He didn't look too good; his face was cut, and a mass of bruises. The air gunner escaped with just slight bruises.

The day after that another plane crashed into the sea. When they picked up the pilot he was without head or legs. He'd only been here training for two days, poor boy. The other crashes were on the runway, but not so serious, just undercarriages ripped off.

Agematsu

After a sleepless night in my body bag tent, I felt too knackered to walk the ten odd kilometers from Suhara to Agematsu and so I took the train. I found a nice *ryokan* called Tamasa, run by another elderly lady, who went about her work leaning heavily on a walking stick.

It was only a twenty-minute walk from there to the Ono Falls, Hiroshige's image to mark the Nakasendō's thirty-eighth post station. The waterfall was disappointing. Once a scenic spot along the Nakasendō, it was now hemmed in from the riverside by Highroad 19 and from above by a massive steel railway viaduct supported by a huge concrete pillar that partly obscured the view.

Halfway to the falls, was the Nezame no Toko Gorge. I was surprised that Hiroshige and Eisen hadn't included the gorge in their series, as it was far more impressive. Over thousands of years the Kiso River has carved its way through a long stretch of bone-white granite, creating a wide crevice some ten meters deep. Flanking the crevice stood a tall granite island, a tiny shrine at its crest.

It was such a peaceful scene that it gave me a start to realize that the impression must have been very different in Hiroshige's day. Then, unhindered by dams, the river must have burst through the crevice with terrible force, shrouding the island, shrine and the whole area in a nebulous haze, not unlike that of the Niagara Falls.

Had it been the haze that had kept Hiroshige and Eisen from depicting the gorge? They certainly must have known about it, for by then the myth of Urashima Tarō, the simple fisherman who visits the palace of the Dragon God under the sea, had already connected itself to the gorge. The leaflet from the Agematsu Town Tourism Association explained:

After returning to our world from the undersea realm of the dragon gods, Urashima Tarō wandered the country before settling in the village of Agematsu where, every day, he enjoyed his favorite activity of fishing in the waters of Nezame no Toko. Above the rocks is the Urashima shrine, where legend has it that Urashima Tarō finally opened the forbidden box gifted to him by the dragon princess and in a puff of smoke instantly aged 300 years.

That night, on my return to the Tamasa *ryokan*, I had a chat with the landlady. Now in her seventies, she recalled how

hard life had been when she was a child. Twice her parents'
house was destroyed by fire, the first time in 1943. The second
time in 1959, when practically the entire village was gutted
by a large fire that began on the town's northern side and
only stopped when it had reached the southern end and
destroyed everything in its way. These had been terribly hard
times for her parents, who somehow had to build a new house,
even though the mortgage for the first one hadn't been paid
off yet. There was no government aid in those days. It was
only fourteen years since Japan's defeat, and the country was
struggling hard to recover from the war's devastation.

I observed that, had it not been for the fire, Agematsu
would still be a village like Magome and Tsumago, attracting
thousands of tourist a year because of its old-time beauty.

It was a shame, she admitted, though living in the old
houses hadn't been all that great. 'They were dark, cold,
damp and generally uncomfortable to live in,' she said. 'So
in that respect I don't miss them a bit.'

Isabella Lucy Bird, the intrepid English explorer, author and
naturalist, who traveled Japan's interior extensively for eight
months on horseback in 1878, describes on many occasions
the harsh living conditions in the more remote areas.
Travelling the impoverished Tōhoku region she notes:

> The houses in this region (and I believe everywhere)
> are hermetically sealed at night, both in summer and

winter, the *amado*, which are made without vents, literally boxing them in, so that, unless they are falling to pieces, which is rarely the case, none of the air vitiated by the breathing of many persons, by the emanations from their bodies and clothing, by the foul air produced by defective domestic arrangements, and by the fumes from charcoal *hibachi*, can ever be renewed.

Exercise is seldom taken from choice and, unless the women work in the fields, they hang over charcoal fumes the whole day for five months of the year, engaged in interminable processes of cooking, or in the attempt to get warm.

Much of the food of the peasantry is raw or half-raw salt fish, and vegetables are rendered indigestible by being coarsely pickled, all bolted with the most marvellous rapidity, as if the one object of life were to rush through a meal in the shortest possible time.

The married women look as if they had never known youth, and their skin is apt to be like tanned leather. At Kayashima I asked the house master's wife, who looked about fifty, how old she was (a polite question in Japan), and she replied twenty-two—one of many similar surprises.

The poor housing, general malnourishment and lack of basic medical care had a terrible effect on the health of rural populations. At Kayashima, a 'miserable village of fifty-seven houses,' just across the border of Fukushima prefecture:

> A little boy, the house master's son, was suffering from a very bad cough, and a few drops of chlorodyne I gave him allayed it so completely that the cure was noised abroad in the earliest hours of the next morning.
>
> By five o'clock nearly the whole population was assembled outside my room, with much whispering and shuffling of shoeless feet and applications of eyes to the many holes in the *shōji*. When I drew them aside I was disconcerted by the painful sight which presented itself, for the people were pressing one upon another, fathers and mothers holding naked children covered with skin disease, or with scald head, or ringworm, daughters leading mothers nearly blind, men exhibiting painful sores, children blinking with eyes infested by flies and nearly closed with inflammation of the eye.

Returning to my room in the Tamasa *ryokan*, I was nevertheless glad today's Japanese hadn't done away with tradition wholesale. I loved the *shōji*, which cast a tempered, white light into the traditional room and alcove, though the thin paper windows were now backed by modern glass. I also liked the *tatami* mats with the *futon* beds, though they might have compromised a bit on the pillows.

Pillows in Japan are invariably hard and too small. It's almost as if they're designed to give you a whiplash, or at least a serious hangover, even after a night without alcohol. I suppose it's a throwback to the times when they were made of small blocks of wood, their only source of comfort a thin strip of velvet across the top. They had come in vogue among *geisha* as a means to keep their elaborate coiffure—which took hours to arrange—in shape for next-day's customer. As for me, I thought the out-of-bed look was a small sacrifice to make.

Rolex

At Kiso-Fukushima station I spotted two men in full traditional Japanese garb, their only modern accessaries small leather clutch bags and Rolex-type watches around their thick wrists. It made me think of my Buddhist friend, Vincent, who had spent many years in Japanese monasteries as part of his research and personal spiritual quest.

At one stage he had been in training at the Honsen-*ji* in Shinagawa, a temple of the Shingon sect when, during a prayer session, he heard a telephone ring among the gathered acolytes. The phone kept on ringing, until one of them reached into his wide sleeves, produced a mobile phone, held it to his shaven head, and whispered something into it between lines of prayer.

Later, unwinding in their private quarters, he spotted another acolyte sporting a golden Rolex, its bright sapphire crystal glass protruding from below the rim of his black sleeve. He had complimented him on his good taste, but immediately came to regret it. The young man reacted as if caught in the midst of some horrible debauchery, turning red enough to change the color of his tanned skin. Casting his gaze down towards the *tatami* in shame, he fumblingly removed the offending symbol of materialism from his sinful wrist as he stammered his excuse, '*Hazukashii naa: hontō no Roorekusu ja nai'n desu; chūgoku no nisemon da*' (This is so embarrassing: it isn't a real Rolex; it's a Chinese imitation).

Torii Pass

I had no meaningful encounters that morning. It was probably because I had been too lazy to travel the old way: by foot. It struck me how in Japan's modern setting many encounters seemed to be fleeting, meaningless, devoid of the human touch. And though everyone was impeccably polite, it was a politeness that seemed sterile, the product of some huge corporate culture. At Seven Elevens, Daily's and what not, people would climb out of their air-conditioned cars, leave the engines running, get their instant noodle or coffee, and consume them in the anonymity of their cabins.

At the entrance to the Torii Pass I ran into Birgitte, a German tourist who had taken three months off to travel through Asia and Russia. She had set a few weeks aside for Japan, after which she intended to cross over to Shanghai, travel inland to visit the Terracotta Army, then to Beijing to camp out on the Great Wall, and back home by way of the Trans-Siberia Express.

She was on her way down, I on my way up, and as we parted she warned me, 'Yuh hef an ahjuos juhney befoh juh.'

She was right enough, the Torii Pass was the toughest bit of walking so far, though still thoroughly enjoyable.

It was roughly at this point that, one hundred years earlier, Kirtland encountered a pilgrim, 'an old man standing before us, leaning on a long staff':

'I was born,' he said, 'in the forty-first year of the rule of *shōgun* Ienari. I was young and am now old. My eighty and seven summers have seen the downfall of the once mighty before the rising to full glory of the Meiji, and now, from the Palace of Edo, shine upon us the divine rays of the Way of Heaven. Great is the mercy of enlightenment. The eternal glory is the Way.

'As a child I knew these mountains which you see. The provinces of our land were then fortified by many castles and these roads were traversed by armed men. The castles have been razed to the ground, but the temples of the gods still stand. The two-sworded warriors have gone but I, a humble pilgrim, still walk the roads they once knew. The white clouds rest in the blue sky above Mount Fuji as when I looked upon them as a child. The clouds will rest above Fuji-*san* when these eyes shall see them not.

'In the fourteenth year of my youth, I took the vow that my life should be lived in honoring the holy images of Buddha, each and all as my steps might find them, from the shrines erected by the peasants to the bronze statues of the great temples. I took the very staff which you see and the clothes that were upon my back and bade my family goodbye. Through the kindness in the hearts of men, the lowly and the mighty, the gods have provided me with food and rest. I have traveled without illness and my spirit has known the joy of the Way.'

Walking through the quiet woods, it was hard to imagine this was once Japan's most busy inland thoroughfare. Back then, a daily stream of travelers and merchants plied the Nakasendō in both directions, thus providing lifeblood to the small communities along the way.

John la Farge, an American painter who traveled Japan in 1886, only a few decades after Japan's 'opening' to the West, gives a good impression of the intensity of traffic on Japan's highroads at the time. Travelling the first leg of the Nakasendō, from Kyoto to Ōtsu, he observed how:

Long trains of beautiful black bulls, drawing lumber or merchandise, or carrying straw-covered bales, streamed peacefully along. We passed peasant women—hardy, tall, sometimes handsome, with scarlet undergowns held up. Occasionally one rides on a packhorse, or in her place a child is perched on the hump of the wooden saddle. Or, again, peasants bearing loads on their backs, or carriers with weighty merchandise swung between them on poles. Priests, young and old, stepped gravely in their white, or yellow, or black dresses—some with umbrellas open, others, whose quicker step meant that they had not far to go (perhaps only to some wayside temple), protecting their shaven heads with outspread fan.

Or a *kuruma*, usually with one runner, taking into town, economically, two women together, one old, one young, and followed by another *kuruma* carrying some old gentleman, very thin or very fat, the head of a family. *Kuruma* carrying Japanese tourists or travelers, with hideous billycock hats, or Anglo-Indian helmets, or wide straw hats à la mode de Third Avenue, these abominable head-pieces contrasting with their graceful gowns, as did their luggage, wrapped up in silk handkerchiefs with their European traveling rugs.

Or, again, other *kuruma* carrying unprotected females in pairs, with the usual indifferent or forlorn look. Or couples of young girls more gaily dressed, with flowery hairpins, the one evidently a chaperon to the other. Then a government official, all European, with hurrying runners. Sometimes, but rarely, the Japanese litter, or *kago*, or several if for a party, their occupants lying at their ease as to their backs, but twisted into knots as to their feet, and swaying with the movement of the trotting carriers. Bent to one side by the heavy ridgepole, which passes too low to allow the head to lie in the axis of the body, sweet-eyed women's faces, tea-rose or peach-colored, looked up from the bamboo basket of the litter. With proper indifference their lords and masters looked at us obliquely. On the roofs was spread a miscellaneous quantity of luggage.

Most of that traffic found its way to Edo along the less taxing Tōkaidō. Those who had to use the Nakasendō to reach their destination were in for a hard slog, especially the itinerant merchants, who literally carried their stores over the mountains on their backs. Travelling Japan's deep interior, Isabella Lucy Bird saw at close hand the hardships they had to endure:

Merchants carrying their own goods from Yamagata actually carry from 90 to 140 pounds, and even more. It is sickening to meet these poor fellows struggling over the mountain passes in evident distress. Last night five of them were resting on the summit ridge of a pass gasping violently. Their eyes were starting out. All their muscles, rendered painfully visible by their leanness, were quivering. Rills of blood from the bite of insects, which they cannot drive away, were running all over their naked bodies, washed away here and there by copious perspiration.

No wonder the Torii Pass was considered such a huge obstacle. Climbing the narrow winding path up towards the pass it was hard to imagine how all that traffic could have negotiated the many hurdles the mountains had in store. Especially the descent must have been treacherous. Even now the path was exceedingly narrow, making sharp turns to follow the mountain's steep and erratic slopes. At several places wooden bridges, simple, planked structures supported by two thick logs on both sides, spanned the deepest crevices.

To those who lived in Narai the Torii Pass was a boon. Aware that it was the most difficult stretch of the Nakasendō, travelers in both directions spent more time at the post town, either to rest their weary limbs or to build up strength for the taxing climb ahead. I fantasized how fascinating it would be to go back in time and see with my own eyes what it had been like in those days.

Aoki-san

When I entered Narai, a large number of uniformed high school pupils were swarming the place.

As I passed one group, I took a photograph of them and a guide in traditional costume handing out some leaflet with information. A few of the children turned and made the usual V-sign, but most regarded me with the same indifference as any other passerby. What a difference with the time I had first arrived in Japan! Had I met them then, I would have been the focus of their attention, not Narai.

Not that I regretted it one bit. I well remember how during the half year I lived in Mobara in the late eighties, classes just out from school would follow me around town calling out, '*Heroo! Heroo! Gaijin!*' It seemed that with each year and the ever growing presence of foreigners this exasperating trait among the Japanese had disappeared.

No wonder the first foreign visitors to travel Japan's interior had such a hard time of it, especially if they happened to be of the fairer sex. Isabella Lucy Bird describes, in the unfrazzled fashion of the true Victorian explorer, the commotion she caused when, in the summer of 1878, resting at the small town of Yuzawa in Japan's Tōhoku region:

> I took my lunch—a wretched meal of a tasteless white curd made from beans, with some condensed milk added to it—in a yard, and the people crowded in hundreds to the gate. Those behind, being unable to see me, got ladders and climbed on the adjacent roofs, where they remained till one of the roofs gave way with a loud crash, and precipitated about fifty men, women, and children into the room below, which fortunately was vacant. Nobody screamed—a noteworthy fact—and the casualties were only a few bruises. Four policemen then appeared and demanded my passport, as if I were responsible for the accident.

From my perspective there was just one vexing aspect to the school classes that had descended on Narai: they were all staying for the night. Consequently, every place was booked to the last room.

In desperation I again turned to the local tourist office for help. The place was run by Mr. Nishizawa Toshio, an avuncular man a few years younger than myself. He said not to worry. There was a place on the edge of town that might take me in. The man who ran it was currently guiding a group of students around, but he would be dropping by presently.

Greatly relieved, I waited on the bench in front of the tourist office and exchanged pleasantries with Nishizawa-*san* on travel and surviving abroad. He spoke pretty good English and even knew a few Dutch words, among them *dankjewel*, which means 'thank you.'

We had been chatting for some time when suddenly he raised his head and beckoned with his hand in the Japanese manner (the palm downward) and called out, 'Aoki-*san!*'

An elderly man, a Japanese version of Sir Michael Gambon, dressed in a guide's *haori*, came sauntering towards us, his beady eyes glaring at me from a deeply furrowed forehead. Around it was tied a *tenugui* (cotton towel), which gave his whole appearance that of a Caribbean pirate.

Nishizawa-*san* introduced me and asked if Aoki-san could put me up for the night.

The old man looked me over and nodded.

How much would it be for a *sudomari*?

Without saying a word Aoki-*san* raised his right hand, then four fingers, then five.

'Four thousand and five hundred yen,' Nishizawa-*san* said with a broad smile in my direction.

I returned his smile and thanked Aoki-*san*, who gave me a curt nod and went on his way.

The Toge no Juku Aoki wasn't far from the tourist office, Nishizawa-*san* assured me. In fact, I had passed it on my way into town. It stood at the foot of the long and winding path down from the Yamatoge Pass.

For a tourist guide Aoki-*san* seemed to resort to few words. But when I reported at his *minshuku* around seven that evening he showed a different, far more cordial side.

Inviting me into his living room and the presence of his wife and another male guest, he poured me a cup of green tea and asked where I was going. I told him and explained the purpose of my journey.

His interest raised, he grew talkative. Did I know, he asked, that his pension was built on the same spot as a comb shop depicted in one of the woodblock prints of the *Sixty-nine Stations of the Nakasendō*?

He began to rummage through one of the old cupboards in his living room and produced a copy of The o-Roku Comb Shop at Narai Station, the thirty-fifth wood-print in the series. Like the one of the bridge over the Ina River, this one was also painted by Keisai Eisen.

I asked Aoki-*san* which of the two artists he preferred.

'Well,' he said, 'Hiroshige's works are very colorful. Eisen's works are a bit more subdued and more in tune with the Japanese sense of sobriety.'

He pointed out how, just behind the comb shop, the path steeply climbs into the mountains. 'That is exaggerated,' he said. 'It's done for dramatic effect. You won't see any mountain paths that steep around here.'

Looking it up afterwards, my maps claimed the shop had been situated closer to town, at the 'entrance' of the path leading up to the Torii Pass. But I was inclined to believe Aoki-*san*. I also loved the poetry of the idea.

The o-Roku hadn't been the only comb shop in Narai. The whole economy of Narai was supported by the age-old implement. It was one big community of artisans churning out combs for the rest of Japan. There were also *nushiya*, artisans who covered the combs in the many layers of highly polished lacquer of the *urushi* tree.

There was a reason, he said, why Narai had become known for its combs. On the slopes around Narai grew the fine-grained hardwoods that were suitable: *minebari* (cherry birch), *yamanashi* (pear tree), *konashi* (crabapple) and *tsuge* (box tree).

These also weren't among the five tree species whose use was banned by the Bakufu in Edo. To control the supply of this important commodity the Bakufu had brought all wood production in the region under direct Tokugawa control. There were three main branches of the Tokugawa clan, known as the Gosanke: the House of Kii, the House of Mito and the House of Owari. It was the lord of the House of Owari that ruled the Kiso Gorge from Magome all the way to Niekawa, a stretch also known as the Kiso Jūichi Juku, the 'Eleven Kiso Posts.'

The Bakufu had even promulgated a special law, the *Goboku Bassai Kinshi-rei*, which made it a crime punishable

by death to fell one of the designated five species (*hinoki,
sawara, asunaro, kōyamaki, nezuko*) without permission.

The wood harvested on the slopes along the Kiso Gorge
was transported all around the country. The huge trunks
were dragged downhill and cast in the Kiso River. Carried
downstream on the river's strong current, they would eventually reach the Bay of Ise, where they were processed and
shipped around the country. It was a huge industry
supplying wood to sites like the famous Ise shrine.

'The Ise shrine still uses wood from here,' Aoki-*san* said.
'Every twenty years, when the shrine is rebuilt, there is a
huge ceremony in which carefully selected trees are felled
for the shrine using special cutting techniques.' With a wry
smile he added, 'Of course nowadays, what with all the dams,
they have to be transported over the road by truck.'

Aoki-*san* also shone a different light on the *sankin kōtai*
system I had discussed with Matsubara-*san* at the old tea
house halfway Magome and Tsumago. It was true, he said,
that it drained the resources of the country's feudal lords.
But this too had been a Bakufu strategy to deplete their war
chests and thus curb their military muscle. It was only when
some of them teetered on the brink of bankruptcy that the
Bakufu finally relented and lengthened the intervals at which
they were required to attend.

Not many lords used the Nakasendō to reach Edo; most
used the somewhat shorter Tōkaidō, which was easier going,
though there were more rivers to cross.

Aoki-*san* had largely built his hostel with his own hands. He had started out as a *nushiya*. It had been a hard trade to learn, not only because of the required skill but more so because the *urishi* resin that is used can cause severe rashes in those who have not been exposed to it. In the old days, he explained, the local children, playing in the woods, would be naturally exposed to the toxins, faint traces of which would be contained in the forest air. Having grown up in the city of Matsumoto, in his case the symptoms had been severe; for months he had suffered from festering scabs in his most sensitive regions that ached unbearably.

Later he had moved into the chemical paint industry. Making good money, he had combed the area around Narai to assemble, bit by bit, the traditional materials from which he would build his *minshuku*. The crowning moment had come when he had persuaded a local farmer to let him reuse the roof of an old and abandoned farmhouse. It still had the old *fukinuke*, an open structure at its apex that allowed smoke from the open fire to escape through the roof while containing much of the fire's heat.

Originally, he went on, all the town's houses were heated in this manner. To further fend off the biting winter cold they were also built close together, which was one of the reasons they were so vulnerable to fire in summer: if one house went up, the whole village did.

It had been thirty years ago now that he had built his own *minshuku*, a task that had taken him three years. He had since closed the roof's aperture. When young, he had gone out into the woods to cut wood for his fire. Now he was too old and he and his wife relied on gas and electricity for their comfort.

I was so taken with Aoki-*san* and his place that I asked him if I could stay another night. It wasn't a problem.

The next evening he knocked on my *fusuma*. Did I care to have dinner at his place, instead of eating out? One of his guests, who was on night shifts, had skipped his dinner, which was now sitting idly on the living room's *kotatsu*.

I readily agreed, and so I spent another pleasant few hours with him and his wife, talking about all kinds of things.

The dinner was the best I had so far on my trip, freshly picked greens and asparagus from the garden, mountain potato, a variety of pickles, stewed squid, braised chicken breast and—best of all—*sashimi* of venison, something I had never had before. He served it with a few thin slices of onion and some freshly grated ginger. It was superb.

I asked him if he had killed the animal himself.

No, he said. And even if he had, one couldn't just eat the meat raw. He had a good friend who had a special refrigerator in which he froze the meat cold enough to kill the parasites that can be found in venison.

In his youth he had done a lot of freshwater fishing, *iwana* (char), *sakuramasu* (masu salmon) and *yamame* (landlocked masu salmon). Now he was getting too old for al the climbing and clambering. But he had found a young *deshi* keen to learn the craft. He also taught him where to find the delicious *sansai*, the 'mountain vegetables,' which are now widely cultivated but can still be found in the wild.

Leaving Aoki-*san* the next morning after a final, freshly made coffee, I felt I had the best part of my trip behind me.

Ichigo Ichie

I spent most of the one rainy day on my trip at Narai, lounging and writing in cafes and restaurants, and talking with the locals. One cafe had a number of electric guitars with beautifully lacquered *urushi*, polished to create a kind of flamed effect. The lady who served coffee said her husband was a *nushiya* and that he had sold many guitars abroad, one to the American guitarist Joe Satriani.

As we were talking we were joined by another foreigner, a tall, good-looking man in his thirties with an athletic build. He seemed restless, occasionally looking over his shoulder, as if he was being pursued.

Intrigued by our conversation he introduced himself as Ted Taylor and complimented me on my Japanese. I requited the compliment, for he spoke Japanese like a native. It turned out he was a tour guide. Originally from New Mexico, he had been living in Japan for almost twenty years now. He was currently leading a group of a dozen tourists down the Nakasendō. Like me they were doing most of it on foot. Eager to know more about the sights, the people in his group were constantly pestering him for information. He realized it came with the territory, but every now and then he had the urge to escape—like now. He had done this stretch of the route close to thirty times and knew the places where he could safely hide. The shop we were in had an almost hidden upstairs room where he could spend some quality time on his own without being noticed.

As we got talking he sat down at my table and we exchanged our various Japan experiences. Both of us had taken up *iaidō*, the Japanese art of fencing, when we had first arrived in Japan. He was a practitioner of the Itoguchi-*ryū*, the school that has its breeding ground in Matsue, the old castle town on the Sea of Japan where Lafcadio Hearn once used to live. He himself was now based in Kyoto, where he divided his time between being a tour guide and writing books on traveling in Japan. He had, among others, done a book on the Shikoku Henrō, the famous but grueling pilgrimage along eighty-eight of Shikoku's temples.

He gave me several bits of good advice for the road. One of them was what he called the 25/25 rule: never walk more than twenty-five kilometers a day when the temperature rises above twenty-five degrees Celsius. I told him I needn't worry, then, as my maximum so far was fifteen.

Though he enjoyed the tours, for him they were mainly a means to an end. He wanted to spend more time writing, but somehow other things always seemed to get in the way. Considering the poor deal one got at established publishers, he was thinking of setting up his own publishing house. Given the burgeoning e-book market and the new print-on-demand businesses model, it was an attractive proposition. He was well connected and knew plenty of other foreign writers on Japan. There were also plenty of Japanese books that could find an English audience when translated. And there was always that urge to divulge one's weird experiences in the Japanese martial arts scene. Of course this would mean utter and total excommunication, so perhaps better wait until he had moved abroad.

In parting he pointed at a calligraphy on the wall under which I had been sitting.

'Now that's appropriate,' he said.

I couldn't agree more. It said, *Ichigo ichie*, a saying believed to have been coined by the sixteenth-century tea master Sen no Rikyū, meaning 'treat every encounter as if it were a one chance in a lifetime.'

To Seba

At Niekawa I got off the train and walked the kilometer or so back towards the spot where Hiroshige had painted the thirty-third station of the Nakasendō. It depicted travelers arriving at the Hatagoya inn. From here I wanted to pick up the trail again towards Hideshio, as there was another place I wanted to photograph two-thirds along the way.

I walked down to the river, but there wasn't a trace of a path, not even a hare's. Climbing up towards the road a woman called out after me, holding in her hands a tourist guide to the Nakasendō I had already in my possession.

She had emerged from an old building I had just photographed. It was a former checkpoint she said, the place where all who traveled along the Nakasendō were required to show their travel permits.

Downstairs, in a small gallery built into the slope down towards the river, was a small but wonderful exhibition of reproductions of the Nakasendō series.

It wasn't so much the woodblock prints that roused my interest as the old photograph on display below them, all of them clearly taken towards the end of the nineteenth century. They were there with the permission of a student from Nagasaki University, who had done research into the Nakasendō and excavated the old photographs from some forgotten archive. They were fascinating. All the depicted places were almost exactly as Hiroshige and Eisen had found them a century before. It went to show once again just how much had been lost over the last odd one hundred years. It was only because people were so poor around here, she said, that so much had been preserved. I said I was glad they hadn't had the money. Even as I said it I realized it an awful thing to say, but luckily she found it very funny.

Before she let me go she took a piece of yellow paper and, taking several rubber stamps, made me the kind of permit the old station would once have issued to those who used the Nakasendō. Fully authorized, I hit the road again.

In fact, I did nothing of the sort. It was raining hard now, and I hurried straight back to the shelter at the local train station. It was occupied by a tiny old woman and a balding, bespectacled man in his fifties dressed in sports gear.

He too was doing the Nakasendō, not on foot, but on his mountain bike. He had departed from Nihonbashi four days earlier and expected to arrive in Kyoto in another four. I asked him what he did about the mountain passes. Even on foot they were a slog, and I couldn't imagine him traversing them on his bike, even if it were a mountain bike. But he said he did, leaving me pondering my hiker's integrity as I waited for my train.

Family

At Seba I found a *minshuku* along the highway to Shiojiri. I entered the *genkan* and called out, '*sumimasen!*' No reply. I repeated my call several times, but still there was no sign of life. After ten more minutes I had basically decided to move on. Just to spite the owners, I shouted '*SUMI-MASEEEN!!*' at the top of my voice and made ready to dash out the front door before my verbal grenade would detonate, when a door opened and a disheveled man appeared. He didn't address me but answered my call by sticking his head back through the opened door and shouted, '*Ooi, okusan!*' (Hey, wife!). A few more minutes and a sullen woman appeared. The moment she appeared the man withdrew, leaving her to show me to my room.

The place had seen its best days long ago. A dark, linoleum-covered hallway led to equally dark rooms with ragged curtains, strategically drawn to hide a view onto what looked like an abandoned junkyard. The only window into a brighter future in the equally drab dining hall was a rusted frame with a faded picture of what must have been their grandchildren.

The landlady blended in seamlessly with her lackluster environment. She was dressed in a worn apron and her hair looked unkempt. On her face she wore an expression as if she was laboring under some constant burden, perhaps an adulterous husband—or one who just sat on his arse all day and let her do all the hard work.

I was just too tired to decline and look for another place and decided to brave it out. At least I would be dry and warm.

The only thing that saved my room from becoming a prison cell was its alcove (*tokonoma*). In it hung a scroll with a seasonal watercolor framed in silk.

That night, looking at the scroll from my bed amid the general gloom, put me in a melancholic mood. I cast my mind back thirty years to my time in Mobara with the Takayanagi family. My plan to land a record contract with one of the major Japanese labels had failed miserably. So had my romance with Naoko. More and more she had recused herself, sending deputy girlfriends in her stead to do the dirty work. This they did with some expertise, especially the last one—so much so that I began to wonder if she had done this more often. At some point she observed, 'The time has gone in which … can just fool around.' Masters of the elliptical phrase, the Japanese have evolved a language in which neither object nor subject have to be stated. But the message was clear enough. I considered it a sign of my growing command of the language that I was able to infer exactly who thought what of whom.

It had left me with just one question: what now? My finances were dwindling fast and there was little outlook on my landing a job as most of my Commonwealth friends had done. Most of them too had meanwhile given up on their original dream. They had been able to fall back on what was frowned upon by the few who had made it as the scoundrel's refuge: teaching English. There is an insatiable appetite among Japanese for English lessons, especially *eikaiwa*, 'English conversation.'

Being half English and a fluent speaker, I thought I could at least land myself a job teaching English to bridge the time till my return home. But the Japanese being who they are needed proof of my qualifications in the form of a passport, i.e., a Commonwealth passport. And thus I set out to acquire one. I eventually managed to get an interview with the English consul. He was kind enough, but told me that with the British Nationality Act of 1981 that avenue had been closed to people like myself. And thus, I seemed deprived of my last refuge, even among scoundrels. There was only one thing left to do: swallow my pride.

Before I had left for Japan my Japanese teacher had urged me to pay the Takayanagis a visit. They lived in Mobara, roughly an hour by train from Tokyo. Mrs. Takayanagi,

Taeko-*san*, was her childhood friend. Her husband, Teruo-*san*, was a *hyōguya*, a scroll-maker. It was still the affluent eighties and he was inundated with work. He said I could help him out. In return, he would pay me five hundred yen an hour and they would provide bed and lodgings.

Bed and lodgings was a bit of an understatement. Sharing one, albeit spacious house with Teruo-*san*'s parents and three children they already had their hands full, but they accepted me as a regular member of the family. Their eldest daughter, Kyōko, even offered up her room for me and moved in with Teppei, their only son, and Minako, the youngest, who were already sharing a room.

For the next five moths, I lived with the Takayanagis as if it had always been that way. We would rise early in the morning for a generous breakfast. Then the children would leave for school, and I would go to help out in the small workshop at the front of the house. Most of my training I received from granddad, as Teruo-*san* was too busy in those days. Granddad was originally from Nagoya and spoke a dialect I only really mastered after I had moved there myself fifteen years later.

Only later did I truly realize it was an experience I could never have had if I had landed a job as a teacher, let alone a record contract. It also taught me the Japanese work ethic, their dedication to quality, their pride in skill.

The first thing I had done on my present trip was visit the

Takayanagis. As always I was warmly welcomed by Taeko-*san* and her children. But there was an aching gap this time. It was five years since Teruo-*san* had passed away, and we all felt it. Their youngest daughter now had children of her own and it was touching to see how much one of them resembled Teruo-*san*.

They put me up in the make-shift guest room, which was separated from the shop by four decorative *fusuma*. Lying there and staring at the empty shop, I still found it hard to wrap my head around the idea that Teruo-*san* wasn't there anymore. Everything was still in place, the low workbenches, the drying boards suspended from the ceiling, the panels with tools and rulers. But something had changed: scrolls were no longer pasted to the drying boards, the benches no longer filled with works in progress.

Shiojiri Pass

The next morning the sun shone, the sky was blue, and the gloom that had haunted me the night before evaporated as if it had never existed. On my way to Seba station, I crossed the road, when an approaching white car pulled up in front of me. It was Nishizawa-*san*, from the tourist office in Narai. He lived in Seba and commuted daily to Narai for his work. To me it felt like a long way to travel, but of course by car it was only a twenty-minute ride.

He asked me where I was headed. I said towards the Shiojiri Pass. He shook his head. 'You're very tough,' he said.

I laughed. The German tourist had told me Torii Pass was arduous, but it had been quite doable.

'Yes, but this one is tougher,' he laughed back.

I again thanked him for fixing me up with Aoki-*san* and we shook hands again. Then he whizzed away in his Toyota hybrid calling out '*Dankjewel! Dankjewel!*' through his lowered car window.

After the previous day's rain, the mountains stood out sharply against a crisp blue sky. With some luck I should reach Fujimi somewhere in the afternoon, so I would have the sun in my back to photograph Mount Fuji. The town of Fujimi was one of the best places to photograph it; indeed, it was how the town had earned its name: 'see Mt. Fuji.' In the old days the mountain could also be seen from Tokyo, but nowadays, with all the smog, days are rare on which you can get a clear glimpse of Japan's iconic volcano.

Kirtland and his companions had also taken this route after they had reached Lake Suwa, and observed that:

> Fujimi is little more than a hamlet. It is tucked away in a fold of the hills off the main paths of the trail. Its days are probably as ancient as the worship of Fuji-san. The view of the sacred mountain from Fujimi is a paradox of the beautiful. The sudden sight of the blue outline of the mountain against the sky comes crushing into one's consciousness as an extraordinary awakening and quickening, and yet the emotion is deep, reverent, and silent.

Nishizawa-*san* had indeed been exaggerating. The Shiojiri Pass wasn't all that hard; compared to the Torii Pass it was a breeze. The road was hardened and the climb and descent far less steep. It was also far less beautiful—except for the view once you reach the top. A specially erected watchtower gives you a majestically panoramic view towards both sides of the Pass. Sadly, that day Mount Fuji was obscured by distant clouds, but for the rest the view was stunning.

On my way down I encountered a group of young lads in uniform. At first I thought it odd, as they looked like navy cadets in training, dressed as they were in white pants and blue tops—but at Kami-Suwa?

They turned out to be a junior high school baseball team, running up to the Shiojiri Pass to test their condition.

They made me think of my time in the military, when one of my favorite sports was beating our *gung-ho* sergeant at the obstacle course, called a *stormbaan* in Dutch. Having always been an outside kid, I was quite good at it, which earned me the dubious nickname of *Sturmbannführer*.

Otherwise I hated the military. It seemed a perfect waste of time, especially since it would cost me a year's worth in study grants. I had set my sights on university and was desperate for a way out. So were a number of my roommates. Being conscripted, we were all fervently anti-military and had our obligatory NO MORE WAR posters attached to what for obvious reasons was called the 'porno ledge.' Yet few of us had a clue how to circumvent this annoying obstacle towards our pacifist future.

One of use, Robert van Wereld, a somewhat withdrawn, introvert guy, said there was a way out. He refused to elaborate, but one day, as we were on yet another futile training mission, he wasn't there. It turned out he had been to the Bureau for Individual Assistance, which catered to soldiers in psychological distress. He said he'd gone through a number of written tests topped by a session with a psychiatrist. He had to wait a week for the results, but he was pretty hopeful. Two weeks later I saw him again. He was in his civvies. He had 'passed' the test with flying colors and was a free man.

I couldn't believe it; was it that easy? I had to find out.

So the next week I stole myself to an off-barracks telephone booth and called the bureau. I had no qualms about doing so—anything to get out. The only thing I dreaded was facing my father if I did. A conservative man with a career in the merchant navy, he wouldn't be too pleased with my dropping out like this.

I had prepared myself as best I could, going over the material with Van Wereld in detail and imagining the questions the shrink might throw at me. I had read about Method acting, and like an up-and-coming De Niro, I immersed myself in my script of experience.

In the end, it was the interview with the shrink that proved hardest, for he didn't seem too convinced ten more months in the army would scar me mentally. He actually said so when I went back the next week for the results. My heart sank; there went my one year's worth of grants.

'However,' he continued, 'in view of the test results we have nevertheless decided to let you go.'

It felt like a triumph at the time. Looking back now, a suicide attempt and three months of institutionalization in my rucksack, I now realize there had indeed been some method in my madness.

Fake Food

Okayama, on the northern shore of Lake Suwa, was the same dump as when I visited it almost ten years earlier. A long string of car dealers, tire centers, Macdonalds, parking lots, concrete apartment blocks, and Vegas-like signboards with flashing neon lettering screamed at me as I walked into town. And then to think how beautiful a town on one of Japan's few large natural inland lakes could be—it was enough to make one want to scream back.

At least along the shore of the lake they had made an effort to green the place up a bit, with long parks lining the shore all the way to the old town of Kami-Suwa.

Halfway Shimo-Suwa wasn't much better. Only the great Suwa Taisha was as magnificent as ever. Flanking the Nakasendō where it enters the Kantō Mountains towards Tateshina, it is one of Japan's oldest shrines, already mentioned in the *Nihon shoki*, the second-oldest extant chronicle of ancient Japan. At the center of a wide court, shaded by a towering cedar tree and flanked by two bronze *komainu* (guardian dogs) on pedestals stood the Lower, Autumn shrine, a massive *shimenawa* (enclosing rope) fit for giants strung across its entrance atop a steep flight of stairs.

Out of pure nostalgia I decided to have lunch at Denny's— a mistake, of course. They used to serve a decent club sandwich when I was still studying in Tokyo. There were still the obligatory skewers (now made of plastic), but they had tried to change a winning team and failed. As if to remove any lingering doubt about their lack of commitment, they had dumped a huge pile of French fries on top of their botched creation. Or was it just to hide it?

Apart from the pasta and meat, it was one of the few dishes on the menu that seemed edible—fit for human consumption, even. Hamburgers were draped in some kind of polyester coating designed to preserve the meat for at least a decade. Indeed, many of the dishes featured on the menu looked more plasticky than the artfully crafted display dishes meant for shop windows. They seemed synthesized, a virtual rendering of what a poppy, big-eyed manga heroine might thrive on. Perhaps that was why I had to patiently wait behind a long line of parents with children. No wonder the average age in Japan was dwindling by the year.

The whole junk food culture has of course been introduced by the Americans. But as with all foreign influences, the Japanese have taken it a step further. It isn't just junk food anymore, it's more like fake food. In that respect the tide seemed right for some cross-fertilization, some pay-back for the culinary holocaust the Americans have wrought abroad. And besides, with its fake news, fake media and fake president, America seemed just ready to now also embrace fake food.

Ticket

A constant solace along the way were the small train stations, which seemed to transport one back in time by half a century. They are still manned by invariably helpful staff, whose sole purpose in life is to help you get on the right train at the right time.

Only once did I become exasperated with the old-fashioned way things are done at times. At Kobuchizawa station I was just in time for the train to Kōfu. A customer at the ticket office seemed to take her time, so I decided to get a ticket from the vending machine. I had done it a thousand times before but must have done something wrong because, even though I had inserted the correct amount, it wouldn't dispense the ticket. Instead the display said, 'Please wait for the station master to resolve the malfunction.' I was getting nervous; I would have to wait at least an hour for the next train, and the clock was drawing dangerously close to the train's departure time.

I waited—along with a long row of people behind me—until a small panel in the wall next to the machine sprang open. The station master's face appeared in the opening and he said, 'please wait a moment.'

I waited some more, but nothing happened. I looked through the prison porthole and saw the man staring at the back of the machine as if he'd never seen one before in his entire life.

Getting slightly annoyed, I leaned in and said, 'Sorry, but I think my train is leaving in two minutes' (I still had to traverse a tunnel to reach my platform).

He didn't respond but kept staring at the machine.

At length, after what seemed an eternity, my money came rattling back, as if I had scored at a pachinko machine—I was back to zero.

Groaning, I walked to the ticket counter, hoping to purchase a ticket from the station master there.

Running back to his booth, the station master leaned through the window, pointed to the wall and said, 'Please purchase your ticket from the vending machine.'

Now I got really irritated. Why couldn't he provide me with one; it had been done before, you know.

He noticed my irritation and offered: 'Well, in that case, please feel free to pay your fare on arrival in Kōfu.'

I thought, *Whatever*! and began to make my way to the platform when he called out after me, 'Please! I need to issue you with a ticket of admission!'

Somehow I did manage to catch the train to Kōfu, but the experience brought one thing home to me loud and clear: I was drawing dangerously close to Tokyo, to its ceaseless restlessness, its obsession with time, its disregard of 'the other.'

Penshion

That day I had walked 26 kilometers while the temperature soared into the high twenties. I had broken Ted Taylor's golden rule, but still felt in good shape when late in the evening I descended on a youth hostel, though I suspected it only called itself that because it was a member of the International Youth Hostel Association. It was more of a *penshion* really, yet another variety in Japan's wide range of choices when it comes to spending the night.

For some reason the homely, cozy, country-like image of the Japanese *penshion* has never appealed to me—it feels contrived, artificial, out of place. Indeed, it is as if even the Japanese guests who stay at these places feel out of their depth and are unable to unwind the way they would in an environment that feels closer to home. In the cramped, carpeted dining rooms, they sit stiffly in their Western-style chairs, behind Western-style tables, self-consciously clutching knives and forks over plates with Western-style dishes—like children staying over against their will with their stern vicar-granddad in Scotland.

Compare that to the confident swagger with which the Japanese male makes his way around a *ryokan* or *minshuku* in his *yukata*, a towel tied around his forehead. Or how the women, dressed in summer kimono fuss over the elaborate make-up of their *kaiseki ryōri*, the traditional multi-course dinners, served up in front of them on low lacquered tables by giggling maids in *tatami*-covered dining halls. All this after they have thoroughly enjoyed a long communal soak (though now separated by sex) in the establishment's spacious *o-furo*. Or, better still, after a nice stroll to the local *onsen* (hot spring) for which the locality is known. No, *penshions* may be the paragon of decency, but they are light years away from the Japanese spirit.

Evert

Having ticked *penshion*s off my list, I had experienced almost the whole gamut of nightly sojourns on offer in Japan, including a monastery. Only once had I stayed the night in a Buddhist monastery. It hadn't been a great experience, but not because there was anything wrong with the place.

I was traveling with Evert, a seventy-year-old gay neighbor of mine back home, who had come out of the closet in his late fifties when still living in Amsterdam, the European capital of Flower Power. He had been married and had a daughter and two sons. It so happened that one of the latter had met a Japanese woman in Amsterdam. He worked in the IT sector and she had an equally well-paying job. And thus, when they decided to get married, they wanted to do so big time. They were going to have the ceremony in Japan. Not just anywhere in Japan, but at the Atsuta shrine in Nagoya. Money didn't seem an issue. Family and friends would be flown in. Knowing of my background as a Japanologist, Evert had asked me to accompany him as his interpreter and general Japan guide.

I had my doubts. Not that I thought he would move on me, the man could hardly walk. I had occasionally helped him with his support stockings, but apart from the occasional innuendo, he was quite innocent. Evert was an incredibly colorful figure, a Falstaffian presence, with a wide beard, a bellowing voice, and long nails as sharp as razor blades. When he did go out, he would don large colored berets like those worn by French artists, matched by equally colorful Tibetan shawls, which he would drape around his neck with a self-defying feminine flourish. With plenty life experience behind his sizable belt, he saw himself as a bit of a guru. And like all self-respecting gurus, he could be unpredictable and quick to make enemies. This was inevitable; no one of any consequence, in his view, could go through life without doing so. Still, I hadn't been to Japan in years, and with a free ticket on offer, I accepted.

And thus, in the summer of 2011, we boarded a plane bound for Tokyo, where the clan would meet before traveling down to Nagoya. They were nice enough. More than nice, really, and that was the worrying bit. Over the next few days, as we all wined and dined in Tokyo's bars and restaurants, lingering doubts about my arrangement of convenience with Evert were gradually reinforced by their occasional remarks—especially when they learned that we would be touring the Ise Peninsula for five days with a rented car.

They weren't outright warnings, just subtle observations, their purport amplified by a sardonic chuckle here, a raised eyebrow there: 'Really? Five days with Evert...', or 'Have you ever traveled with him before?'

The first two days of our trip were great. Following the coast from Nagoya we visited the Ise shrine. We found a cheap hostel near Owase and from there drove down to the famous Kumano shrine with its beautiful waterfall. Evert was in high spirits and we took turns driving the big Toyota SUV he had rented. I was almost beginning to believe his family were a bit paranoid—were it not for the hit-and-run he committed on the third day.

We had just left Kumano and were entering the mountainous interior of the Ise Peninsula when we came to a small village. A minivan stood parked on our side of the road, right at the center of the village, where the road made a sharp bend towards the left. The van's back doors were open and a woman was unloading cardboard boxes and carrying them into the shop. It was a busy road and, given the sharp bend and the minivan, it was hard to spot oncoming traffic. I assumed Evert would stop, so I could get out and direct him round the obstacle. But he didn't. He didn't even brake, but just carried on. We were about to pass the minivan when a truck came thundering towards us from around the bend. In panic Evert careened to the left, missing the truck by a hair's breadth, but hitting the mirror of the minivan, which broke off and fell to the ground.

Evert still didn't stop. To celebrate our lucky escape, he hit the throttle and sped off into the mountains.

I couldn't believe what had just happened. Thankfully, he hadn't caused any personal injury. But causing material damage to another person's possessions is a grave offense in Japan. To cause damage and simply drive off is enough for any Japanese to seriously consider ritual suicide were he or she to be caught and exposed to public scorn and the eternal shame brought upon one's family and friends.

I pulled the handbrake hard. We came to a screeching halt. Evert looked at me with stupefaction: 'What did you do that for?'

On our return to the shop the woman wasn't angry. She probably thought it was normal for Europeans to simply drive on when they had wrecked another's car. I could only imagine the dim view she must have of traffic on European roads, let alone of those who did the driving. She didn't even insist on reporting the incident to the police; as long as we got her mirror replaced, she was good. We drove both cars to a nearby garage, where, after some checking, the owner concluded he could fix the damage for ten thousand yen. Miraculously, our own mirror didn't have a scratch.

Due to our little incident we were late for our next appointment. That morning, with much trouble, I had managed to make a last-minute booking at the ancient temple complex on Mount Kōya, at the heart of the Ise Peninsula.

For hours we traversed Ise's mountainous interior. After some seven hours behind the wheel, we had finally reached the mountain. With each sharp turn of the road we thought we had arrived, only to find that there was yet another steep ascent, yet another peak lying in wait for us. I was beginning to understand why Mount Kōya had never been conquered like the other great temple complexes of the Ishiyama Hongan-*ji* and Mount Hiei.

At one stage it looked like we had lost our way. It was already dark now and there were next to no road signs. Nor could we rely on our senses. We had made so many twists and turn on our way up that I had lost all my sense of orientation. I simply didn't have a clue where we were.

It was approaching midnight when we reached a few houses along the roadside. I knocked on one of the doors and asked for directions. Luckily, the temple was very near. But hadn't we asked, I was sure we would have missed it.

The temple's abbot wasn't amused when we finally presented ourselves. But in good Japanese tradition he welcomed us and offered us tea.

As soon as I could, I sped off to the toilet to take a leak I had been holding up for several hours, while one of the acolytes showed Evert his quarters.

When I returned Evert was back at the entrance and railing at the abbot: 'Who the hell put me up in this room? It's miles away from the entrance! Can't you see I'm handicapped? I demand a place near the entrance!'

As the interpreter designate, I tried hard to keep up with the diatribe, dropping in the occasional honorific expression so as not to rile the abbot too much.

'Would the honorable abbot be so kind as to consider allocating my client a room closer to the entrance?' I asked.

Frowning, the abbot said, 'I'm sorry to say that all our rooms are occupied.'

'Bugger him. I want a different room,' came the reply.

'Is there no way my client can possibly have a different room,' I humbly proffered, my hands joined together as if in Buddhist prayer. I had been here before in my work: I was going from being a mere 'interpreter' to being a 'cultural interpreter.' It was a dangerous path to tread.

'Is that really what he is saying?' the abbot demanded as he looked passed me doubtfully at a fuming Evert.

I nodded it was, which was true enough if one took into consideration the vast cultural divide that was at play.

But the abbot wasn't buying it. He waved his hand in front of his face, a clear sign that a Japanese wants to avoid any further contact. 'Please tell the honorable guest that we cannot accommodate his wishes.'

Sensing the abbot's irritation, Evert wanted to know what he had said.

By now I had begun to seriously lose my cool. Reversing the same filter I had applied the one way, I translated the abbot's words to a phrasing more in tune with Evert's sensibilities: 'He says you are a pain in the ass.'

It didn't help. Evert now launched into an expletive-filled diatribe against all that was wrong with Japan, gesturing vehemently with his arms and hands, his long nails flailing dangerously close to the paper windows.

Roused by the commotion, half the monastery had been woken and a dozen monks had rushed towards the *genkan*. They were now crowding around their abbot, as they would have in the olden times, when their monastery had been a vast fortress, defended tooth and nail against a hostile world.

I saw only one way out of the mess: intimidation. I had told him earlier how Japanese monasteries had a proud martial tradition, especially Mount Kōya. He had been surprised to hear this, as it clashed with his guru view of Zen. He had also been impressed, slightly fearful even, of staying in such a potentially dangerous environment.

'If you want to leave this place in one piece,' I said, 'you had better tone down your rhetoric a notch.' It worked. His last act of defiance was that he wouldn't be attending Buddhist service next morning.

Woken at six by a priest, I attended morning prayers. Evert was still snoring in his corner of the room. Sunk in meditation I reflected on the last few days and realized I had fallen into the same old trap again: I had been too accommodating, too eager to please. I had done it with my dad, my boss at the cardboard factory, Naoko…

A deadly silence reigned as we drove down to Nara. When we reached Nara's youth hostel I told Evert our roads were parting. He would be fine: it wasn't a long drive back to Nagoya, where his sons were still staying. Of course he disagreed, accusing me of abandoning a helpless old man. But I didn't care anymore.

It was the typhoon season, and Typhoon Roke had made its way up from the Philippines and landed on Japanese shores the day we had left Kumano. We had been lucky. The previous morning, only hours after we had passed through, a large landslide had swept away part of a small village. By now the storm had also reached Nara. As I made ready dense rain was already pelting the youth hostel's large windows. It was fine with me. Putting on my hat and strapping on my rucksack, I stepped out into the sweeping rain and began to walk towards Kyoto. I was drenched within minutes but felt as if I was being cleansed.

I never saw Evert again. Before we had left for Japan, he had bought an apartment in Amsterdam. When I returned home a week later, he had moved.

One year later a beautiful woman moved into Evert's house. She now is the love of my life. She wrote to him once concerning some maintenance contract she had taken over, mentioning in passing that she had grown very fond of his former neighbor. He wasn't amused. He sent back a curt to-the-point letter which he ended on the note: 'And I am NOT AT ALL interested in the affairs of my ex boy-friend.'

I had a lot of explaining to do that day.

Hibakusha

The closer I was getting to Tokyo, the more fleeting also grew the encounters. The same vacant stare I had observed at the convenience stores along the inland highways seemed to gradually return; people became less responsive, exchanges more commonplace. Every now and then someone would ask me where I had come from, where I was headed, but more out of politeness than a genuine interest in who I was or what I was up to. It was as if people gradually began to lose their identity, slowly blending into a crowd that, by the time I entered Tokyo, had reached such a density and uniform consistency that it seemed the individual no longer existed.

At a crossroads west of Shinjuku station, one of Tokyo's major transport hubs, I ran into a young man collecting money for the victims of the 2011 Tsunami. They weren't so much the direct victims of the tsunami—most of them didn't survive. Rather, they were the people whose homes had been contaminated following the explosion of the Fukushima nuclear power plant's third reactor.

In an eerie throwback to the traumatic post-war years, the survivors of the disaster are referred to as *hibakusha*. There are two spellings of the same word, one referring to those who have been exposed to a (nuclear) bomb blast, the other to (nuclear) radiation. These people are victimized in more than one way. Not only have many of them lost their homes and loved ones, living in a highly conformist society, they are also discriminated against. Cars with Fukushima license plates have been scratched or denied service at gas stations; at school children from affected areas are often bullied; many young women have difficulty finding a partner because they might give birth to a child with defects.

After more than six years, the man explained, many of the *hibakusha* were still living in the emergency shelters erected in the immediate aftermath of the catastrophe.

I asked him if the government was helping out, as they had been partly to blame for their failure to prevent errors in design and the poor handling of the crisis.

There had been aid, he said, but now, with the 2020 Tokyo Olympics on their mind, the Fukushima 'issue' had once more disappeared into the background. As a result the various schemes to permanently house the dispossessed were running into serious delays.

On top of this the government had announced that, as of March 2017, they would end housing support for those outside the designated areas, forcing many to return to heavily contaminated homes in and around the ghost towns. Some had refused and become homeless. The Japanese Volunteer Association was helping the victims by raising funds and by putting pressure on the government to do more and do it more expediently.

I told him to keep up the good fight and shoved a thousand yen bill into the cardboard box around his neck, but still felt cheap. How is it, I wondered, that a country that can host the Olympics to the tune of two trillion yen cannot take care of its own people?

Kriegsbewaltigung

In front of Shinjuku station stood the vans of the Uyoku Dantai, Japan's far-right ultra-nationalists. Huge megaphones were blaring out their perennial xenophobic rant against the audio backdrop of the Japanese national anthem.

Sticking my fingers in my ears, I quickly walked on and thought of the time I had attended a fencing rally in one of Nagoya's large sports arenas. The event had been opened with a greeting to the *hi no maru*, the national flag, while the national anthem was being played over the venue's speaker system. I felt queasy about saluting a flag that had arrogantly waved over so much suffering during the Second World War, but that morning I felt especially awkward.

We had been practicing hard the previous day at our *dōjō* when I overheard two of our elderly members fondly reminiscing about what sounded like a holiday they had once been on together. But then I picked up phrases oddly out of keeping with what I had assumed was their subject matter:

'...kicked them out alright...' and 'Weren't those women fun!' I could not help myself as I began to concentrate more closely on their conversation, even moving around to their side of the *dōjō* so as to better hear. They were talking about their days in Singapore, how they had cycled down the Malay Peninsula and kicked out the English.

Judging by their animated conversation they clearly had a terrific time—none of the tortuous *Kriegsbewaltigung* that had preoccupied so many Germans of their age.

I had felt a cheat when I quietly refrained from singing the national anthem. Not that I knew all its lines by heart, but that morning I didn't even make an effort. Nor had I confronted the elderly men about their good old days in Singapore. Were those women who had been such 'fun' perhaps comfort women? It was slowly dawning on me that the Japanese tendency to gloss over their burdened past was especially rampant among those who cherished old traditions—like the ancient art of Japanese swordsmanship.

Not all practitioners were like that. My old teacher in Tokyo, albeit perhaps less thorough than the Germans, had made an effort to reflect on this troubled period.

We had been eating out one night in one of the many small restaurants around Seijōgakuenmae, when he fell silent and grew pensive, as if weighing something in his mind. Then he reached into his coat pocket and handed me a small envelope with the words: '*Tabun kore wa itsuka sankō ni naru*' (Perhaps this might serve as a reference someday).

It contained a short article he had written for a local paper, in which he recalled his memories of the war:

I was woken by my mother's tense voice: 'It's terrible! We're at war with America.'

It was the morning of December 8, 1941.

Having heard that we had started a war with America, I didn't, as one would expect, do my homework. Instead, there being no school that day, my friends and I spent the rest of the day hanging around the Imperial Palace and Ginza. From the electric public bulletin boards, we learned that Japan had launched an all-out air raid on Hawaii.

A crowd had formed on one of Ginza's street corners, around a radio broadcasting a speech by Prime Minister Tōjō Hideki.

In his usual loud voice he was blaring that the whole nation should have faith in certain victory, etc.

But the expression on the faces of the gathered adults was grim and dark.

I too couldn't help wondering if we could ever win just through our 'faith in certain victory.'

In December 1943, he had joined the Imperial Japanese Navy Air Service.

He was trained to be a navigator on a Mitsubishi G4M attack bomber. It was popular among the Japanese strategists for its long range, but notorious among the crews for its total lack of protective armor. To further reduce weight and extend its range, its designers had even done away with the life-saving, self-sealing fuel tanks of earlier models, a feature that soon made it very popular among Allied fighter pilots, who Christened it the Flying Zippo, as its wings only needed a light strafing to set the whole thing ablaze.

Shortly before enlisting, he had asked his father, an English lecturer at Waseda University, about Japan's prospects:

'I don't think we can win from America economically. But if the war drags on and the enemy's casualties rise, America being a material civilization, they might just grow weary of fighting and want to end the war,' my father said having thought long and hard.

'However, when I was studying in America,' he continued, 'the First World War broke out and America finally joined. At that time too morale in America was high and in no way inferior to that in Japan. I think it's dangerous to believe that this time around they will lose the will to fight simply because they've suffered some losses,' he said, his face somber.

Looking back I now realize that my father at that time was a deeply worried man, whose concern for the fate of his country and his son's life were one and the same thing.

With defeat came new insights:

I wasn't only astonished at the great military, technical and economic gap between Japan and America. Though I had been told America was a materialistic country, I now realized just how much they valued human life.

My sorrow for all my friends and peers who had been killed in action grew even deeper.

Having reflected on a senseless war, as well as having enjoyed shrewd policy guidance under the American occupation, the Japanese have turned their backs on the 'strong country; strong army' policy pursued since the Meiji period. And while it has been criticized abroad as an 'economic animal' Japan has since dedicated itself to economic recovery and personal happiness.

Now, celebrating fifty years of peace and prosperity, we are an economic superpower, and Japan's leaders smilingly pledge large amounts of aid to leaders of developing countries visiting Japan.

But recently I have been worrying again, whether we may have forgotten something important along the way, whether we really face a rosy future if we continue on the current path.

Capsule

I had always wanted to try a capsule hotel, and since I wanted to spend the night in Tokyo, I checked in at one in Shinjuku. The immediate association for me was that of space travel. I expected my pod to fill up with the preservative fluids that allowed me to hibernate in a coma-like state until we would reach our destination at some colony lightyears away from earth.

For the space traveler far away from home and loved ones, all their yearnings were catered for: on the cabin's internal screen a young couple were copulating on a couch, on another channel the imperial couple were laying a wreath at some memorial.

The people who populated this spaceship of sorts would not have looked out of place on Ripley's doomed vessel in *Alien*. Checking in at the counter were a motley crew of space hobos, dreamers mostly, hoping to land a fortune on some distant colony. I spotted an almost albino-like white man, bald except for a neatly braided tassel of blond hair that sprang from the back of his head and nervously jumped up and down as he bowed profusely to make up for his poor grasp of the vernacular in this neck of the galaxy. Waiting alongside me for the lift to an upper deck, a young Asian man with long graying hair was dressed in what looked like a coarsely woven Tibetan *chuba*. He was sunk in meditation, a blissful smile illuminating his wide face. In the spacious Neo-Grec style bathroom on deck three a space cowboy with pierced nipples was scrubbing himself down as if to cleanse himself of some contaminating intergalactic dust. I didn't speak his language, but could read the Chinese saying tattooed down the spine of his muscular back: 'Those who enter through the gate of error will find eternal bliss.' I could only imagine the kind of outrages he had committed in the distant regions outside the rule of law.

As always there were those who didn't really belong. On the way down I shared the lift with a young Japanese graduate. He had studied commerce and was now engaged in *shūshoku katsudō*: finding a job.

I slept terribly that night. Not because my capsule was too small, but because the hotel had strategically been built above a live venue. And—lucky us!—that night they were staging a music festival. From roughly midnight till four o'clock in the morning, I got the full encyclopedic treatment of Japan's grunge music scene. Not that it stopped at four.

That was merely the time I decided I had a reasonable grasp on the material and went down to the reception desk to ask for a more quiet berth.

Mosaics

The next morning I rendezvoused with Endō-*san*, my old Tokyo fencing teacher's most senior student. We had arranged to meet outside the Kinokuniya bookstore, an old Shinjuku landmark for foreigners. It was ten years since we had last met, and she worried I might not recognize her. I didn't worry too much; at least she would be able to tell a foreigner from her fellow countrymen.

The last time we had met, we had both joined our old teacher for a light lunch at a sushi restaurant within walking distance from his old house in Seijō. Satake-*sensei* was a very old man now. He had long since laid down his sword, but she said his mind was still razor sharp. He would probably be moving into a special care clinic come summer.

In her sixties herself, she had by now reached the sixth *dan* and annually traveled to Italy to teach a steadily growing group of followers. She enjoyed the trips immensely, not so much because of the teaching but the chance to get away and experience a different country and culture. She was an admirer of Italian art and architecture and loved to visit the country's many old churches with their breathtakingly beautiful mosaics, the Mausoleo di Galla Pradica in Ravenna, the Basilica of San Vitale.

She had become quite proficient in Italian and loved to converse with the locals in their own language about their art and food.

I admired her for her spirit, her sense of adventure. She was someone who had come close to the top of her game. But that wasn't what drove her. It was clear that her command of Japanese swordsmanship had become an occupation, a vehicle to achieve things that were closer to her heart, things that made it beat faster.

Full Circle

So I had finally come full circle; I was in Tokyo and looking back on a journey I had wanted to make ever since I first set foot in Japan almost thirty years ago. Why I didn't do it before I'm not sure. I suspect I subconsciously wanted it to coincide with a stage in my life where it could become the hatching ground for something more than just a fun trip along the sights.

Inevitably, I had seen a lot of ugliness. Yet at various stages along the Nakasendō, well away from the gradually encroaching spread of modernization, I had found vestiges of a different Japan, a place where people had time for each other, where they were interested in each other's stories. They felt like small sanctuaries, time capsules of a world we no longer seem to inhabit.

Oddly, many of the places depicted by Hiroshige and Eisen, too, had been miraculously preserved. It seemed as if they were protected by a force field that even the march of progress dare not touch, as if they were hallowed grounds, inhabited by the spirits of distant ancestors.

My goal was to find some beauty along the Nakasendō. In the end I found something else, something more tangible, a real sense of what the country and its inhabitants once were like—what they were still like, but only in places untouched by the constant march of 'progress.' Looking back, I wonder whether this was what I had been looking for in the first place. I suppose I just had to travel the road first to really find my goal; but then again, as my good Buddhist friend always tells me: 'It's not about the Goal but the Road we travel to get there.'

Glossary

amado:	Sliding shutter.
anjin:	navigator.
asunaro:	*Thujopsis*, a conifer in the cypress family.
bezaisen:	Edo period coastal trader.
daimyō:	Feudal lord.
dan:	Degree of proficiency in Japanese arts.
deshi:	pupil.
dōjō:	Training hall.
eikaiwa:	English conversation.
fukinuke:	Aperture in the roof of a traditional house for the escape of smoke from open fires.
futon:	Quilt.
gaido:	Guide.
gaijin:	Alien.
genkan:	Entrance.
gentaiken:	Life-changing experience.
hakama:	Skirt-like trousers.

hanshi:	The highest of the three budō classes of *renshi*, *kyōshi* and *hanshi*.
hibachi:	Small Japanese charcoal heating appliance somewhat resembling a brazier.
hinoki:	Japanese cypress
hōba:	*Magnolia liliiflora*, or Magnolia.
hyōguya:	Mounter of scrolls, *fusuma* and *byōbu*.
iaidō:	Japanese swordsmanship.
irasshai:	Welcome.
irimoya:	Hip-and-gable roof.
iwana:	Char.
izakaya:	Japanese pub.
jidōhanbaiki:	Vending machine.
kaiseki ryōri:	Multi-course Japanese diner.
kakeudon:	Udon noodles in hot soup.
kawadome:	Times during Japan's feudal era when it was forbidden to cross or ford a river.
kawagoshi:	River-crossing.
kinoko:	Mushroom.
kokudama:	National treasure.
komainu:	Lion-shaped guardian dogs.
konashi (zumi):	*Malus sieboldii*, a species of crabapple.
kōri:	Ice.
kotatsu:	Heater attached to the bottom of a low table and covered with a thick quilt.
kōyamaki:	*Sciadopitys verticillata*, or Japanese umbrella-pine.

kuruma:	Vehicle.
kyūri:	Cucumber.
mawarimichi:	Detour.
minebari:	*Betula grossa*, or Japanese cherry birch.
minshuku:	Japanese-style bed and breakfast.
miso:	Seasoning of fermented soybeans with salt and *koji* (the fungus *Aspergillus oryzae*).
mochi:	Rice cake made of glutinous rice.
nasu:	Eggplant.
nezuko:	*Thuja Standishii*, an evergreen coniferous tree in the cypress family.
ninsoku:	Laborer.
noren:	Sign curtain hung at shop entrance.
nushiya:	Artisan working with paint made from the resin of the *urushi* tree.
o-aisō:	The bill.
o-furo:	Bath.
okusan:	wife.
onigiri:	Rice ball filled with savory filling and wrapped in *nori* (seaweed).
onsen:	Hot spring.
penshion:	Pension.
ryokan:	Japanese-style hotel.
sakuramasu:	masu salmon.
sankin kōtai:	Bakufu policy by which *daimyō* were required to spend alternate years in their domain and the capital of Edo.

sansai:	Mountain vegetables.
senbei:	Rice cracker.
sensei:	Teacher.
shikkui:	Japanese eggshell stucco.
shimenawa:	Twisted straw rope with stripes of zigzag-shaped white paper streamers (*shide*) that are hung around an object to ward off evil spirits.
shōji:	Latticed window covered with translucent paper.
snakku:	Bar.
sudomari:	Stay overnight without meals.
sukebe:	Pervert.
sumimasen:	Excuse me.
tenugui:	Cotton hand towel.
tsuge:	*Buxus microphylla*, or Japanese box.
urushi:	Lacquer made from the resin of the *Toxicodendron vernicifluum*, or Japanese sumac tree.
yakisoba:	Fried noodles.
yama:	Mountain.
yamame:	Landlocked masu salmon.
yamanashi:	*Pyrus pyrifolia*, or Japanese pear tree.
yukata:	Cotton summer kimono.
zarusoba:	Chilled buckwheat noodles served with a cup of cold dipping sauce.

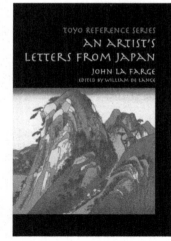

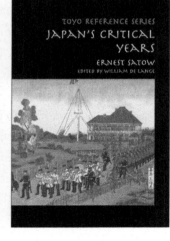

TOYO PRess: Explore Dream Discover
Editorial supervision: Letitia van der Merwe.
Drawing: John de Lange. Book and cover design:
Chōkei Studios. Printing and binding: IngramSpark.
The typefaces used are Cardo and Prescript.